I BELIEVE

Now
Tell
Me
Why

I BELIEVE

Now Tell Me Why

Though this book is designed for group study, it is also intended for your personal enjoyment and spiritual growth. A leader's guide is available from your local bookstore or from your publisher.

Beacon Hill Press of Kansas City
Kansas City, Missouri

Editor
Everett Leadingham

Editorial Assistant
Bryan Merrill

Editorial Committee
Randy Cloud
Everett Leadingham
Thomas Mayse
Stephen M. Miller
Carl Pierce
Gene Van Note

Copyright 1994
by Beacon Hill Press of Kansas City

ISBN 083-411-5182

Printed in the United States of America

10   9   8   7   6   5   4   3

CONTENTS

A WORD ABOUT THIS BOOK

SOMETIMES IT'S UNCOMFORTABLE being a theologian. When folks today use the word *theologian* or *theology*, what follows is not generally a compliment.

We live in an antitheological day. Perhaps it's a reaction to generations of teaching that often told us what to believe but not always why.

Though the mere mention of theology repels people—and is why the word doesn't appear on the cover of this book—almost everyone is a theologian. Theology is not revelation from God. It is seldom inspired. And it is never inerrant. Theology is a human endeavor.

The very word *theology* comes from two Greek root words meaning a discourse or discussion (*logos*) about God (*theos*).

So anyone who says anything about God is a theologian.

The question is not whether we will be theologians. The question is what kind of theologians will we be? Will our theology—our discussion about God—be biblical, logical, consistent, and true to the experience of Christians? Or will it be self-serving, narrow, and contradictory? Will our theology make sense in every portion of Scripture and every circumstance of life? Or will it fit only special circumstances and selected parts of the Bible? Will we be good theologians or sloppy ones?

We want you to be good theologians.

We also want you to understand what it means to be a Christian in the Wesleyan theological tradition. In the world around us there are Christians from many theological families: Roman Catholic, Eastern Orthodox, Lutheran, Reformed (including Calvinists), Anabaptist, Charismatic, and Wesleyan*, to name a few. Each group speaks with its own accent and contributes important ideas to the theological discussion of all Christians.

This book is written by Wesleyans for Wesleyans.

Wesleyans are not just Baptists who believe in sanctification or Charismatics who don't speak in tongues. Wesleyans, including churches like Church of God (Anderson), Church of the Nazarene, Evangelical Friends, Free Methodist Church, Salvation Army, and The Wesleyan Church, have a different way of thinking about God, sin, human beings, the Bible, and salvation. It is not so different that we end up talking only to ourselves, but our accent, emphasis, and favorite themes are not the same as those in other theological families.

Our Wesleyan churches have many members who have only recently joined the church. They were raised in different theological families. Some were theological orphans and raised without a family of faith. That's one of the reasons we wanted to produce this book—to welcome newcomers into the Wesleyan faith by explaining our emphases.

There's another reason. Many of our longtime members have heard theological discussion from folks of other theological families. So this book is offered to our old-timers as a refresher course.

Quite frankly, there is yet another reason for this book. The contributors are concerned that the Wesleyan way of thinking and talking about God not disappear. I've seen such things happen.

My great-grandfather Hahn came to the United States from Germany in 1848. He spoke only German, and he married a German-speaking girl. Their son, my grandfa-

---

*When the word "Wesleyan" is used throughout this book, it will refer to the Wesleyan theological tradition, whose founder is John Wesley. If reference is made specifically to the Wesleyan denomination, then the title "The Wesleyan Church" will be used.

ther Hahn, grew up hearing German at home but English at school and in the community. He married a girl who did not speak German. Their son, my dad, grew up knowing no German at all. I had to learn German by taking classes.

In two generations, a family's ability to speak and understand their native German language disappeared.

The Wesleyan family could lose its distinctive language and accent just as easily.

In the last 40 years, theologians from many different theological families have started paying attention to the insights of John Wesley, our theological forefather. After two centuries of being ignored and put down as a preacher rather than a theologian, Wesley is now recognized by other theological families as a significant scholar who rediscovered important biblical principles relating to the concept of holiness. It would be tragic if the Wesleyan family were to forget its language right at the time other families are beginning to listen and wanting to learn.

This book is unique in that each chapter is the shared work of theologians and journalists. All the theologians teach in the religion department of a Wesleyan denomination's liberal arts college. The journalists teach in the journalism department of a different college in the Wesleyan tradition.

The teaming up of theologians with journalists is an attempt to provide two things. We wanted each chapter to contain the best theology this publishing effort could produce. (That was the theologians' job.) We also wanted laypersons to be able to read and understand each chapter. (That was the journalists' job.)

We don't know of any other book ever produced this way.

The theologians were sure they knew how to write for laypersons. The journalists were sure they knew good theology. Both were a bit surprised.

The discussion was spirited. Sometimes we even agreed. We are all Wesleyans. We all love the Lord. And we all care intensely about our faith. We are still discussing.

Now we invite you into the discussion. May your thinking, discussing, and sharing your faith enliven your relationship with Christ.

ROGER HAHN
Chair, Department of Religion
Southern Nazarene University
Bethany, Okla.

A WORD OF APPRECIATION

I HAVE A THEORY.

The harder an editorial project is on the writers and editors, the better it is for the readers.

If that's true, you're in for a treat—because this has been a very challenging book to put together.

First, we wanted to translate our basic Christian teachings into a different language: English. "Christianese" would not do.

Second, we decided to accomplish this by teaming theologians with journalists. We didn't expect the theologians to be experts in English or the journalists to be experts in the Bible.

Well, it is finished. The translation is complete, and the theologians and journalists never did come to blows.

I'd like to thank all the contributors for their commitment to presenting our people with sound theology in clear English.

Special thanks go to Roger Hahn, who led the team of theologians, and to Dean Nelson, who led the journalists and who provided additional assistance in editing the book. Both men helped create the idea from thin air, then gave the idea words.

Editor

THE CONTRIBUTORS

Theologians, from the religion department of Southern Nazarene University, Bethany, Okla.

Dennis Bratcher, associate professor of religion

Frank Dewey, Garner chair of missions, 1992-93

Don Dunnington, academic dean, and vice president of academic affairs

Howard Culbertson, associate professor of missions and religion

W. Stephen Gunter, professor of religion

Roger Hahn, chair of the Department of Religion and Philosophy, and professor of religion

Wes Harmon, associate professor of philosophy and missions

Sam Harris, adjunct professor of religion

Lyle Pointer, assistant professor of religion

Jirair Tashjian, professor of religion

Journalists, from the journalism program of Point Loma Nazarene College, San Diego, Calif.

Karen DeSollar, director of communications

Vicki Hesterman, associate professor of journalism

Dean Nelson, associate professor of journalism

The Short Course

The Image of God

God created us with the capacity to love Him and others. It's built into the fabric of life in every man, woman, and child.

Humanity's First Sin

The desire to be in charge of their own lives alienated humanity's first parents from God. This desire has also alienated each person from God since then.

Our First Love

God's image within each of us draws us to want to be like our original parents—perfect in love toward God and one another.

BACKGROUND
SCRIPTURE:
Gen. 1:26-31; 3:1-20
Ps. 8:3-8
Matt. 22:36-39

W. Stephen Gunter
and
Dean Nelson

1

It's Human Nature

Don't let the morning news get to you. There's reason to be hopeful.

THERE IS SOMETHING WONDERFUL about being a human being. It might not always seem that way, like when we find ourselves in a yelling match at home or in a political tug-of-war at work. But even in the middle of an imperfect world, we can experience wonder in our humanity.

Like the Psalmist, we can look around us and see the minutest intricacies of nature as well as the vastness of the star-spangled universe. And overwhelmed we, too, can ask, "What is man that you are mindful of him . . . ?" (8:4). For as overpowering as creation is, God has made human beings just a little less than God. He has given us mastery over all creation. He has even given us the power to become creative ourselves.

Think about the creative nature of the human being. Not that long ago, we traveled on land by horse and buggy. We traveled on the ocean by wooden boats, many of which are now on the ocean floor between continents. And we communicated by letter and telegraph.

But now we can travel by hurtling through the air, crossing an ocean in a matter of hours instead of months. We can launch ourselves into outer space, walk on the moon, send expeditions to Mars, communicate by telephone, computer, fax, and satellite.

How is it possible that finite and fallible people like us

could accomplish so much so rapidly? What is the secret to the incredible capacity of our minds? Are there any limits to our discoveries, and can this creativity and ingenuity continue until the end of time?

The Bible does not answer all these questions, but it does tell how we came into being and why we are the way we are.

How We Humans Got the Way We Are

Think about the relationship our first parents had in the Garden of Eden. It is easy to imagine that in the early days of their life they were "lovebirds," like so many new-lyweds today. They likely delighted in the discovery of one another and in all the joys of their intimacy. Perhaps they talked by the hour and were deeply satisfied with the open and honest communication they shared. Neither of them probably ever thought they were loved less than 100 percent by the other. Yet they were totally and completely and absolutely human. And that was good.

That is how God made human beings—good.

When God the Creator looked at all of creation, including humanity, the verdict was decidedly positive: "God saw all that he had made, and it was very good" (Gen. 1:31). This was God's perspective at the end of the sixth day of creation. He was so pleased that He took the next day off and declared it the Sabbath, the day of rest.

In a world that has long since lost its resemblance to the Garden in paradise, it is hard to envision how good it was. There is too much pain and evil all around us. Yet even in this weed patch in which we live we can catch glimpses of what the world was once like. We can see it in human creativity, ingenuity, our capacity to care, communicate, and love. These are some of the basic elements that make us human.

Where did we get them? The Bible is clear about that.

Our essential nature—that which makes us human—comes from God. We were made like God: "Then God said, 'Let us make humankind in our image, according to our likeness'" (Gen. 1:26, NRSV).

In the ancient world it was common to say that kings were "in the image of God." But the creation story is much more generous. All of us are made in God's image. There is not one human being who is without this essential tie to God. But what does this mean?

In the Image of God

The "image of God" that the Bible talks about most likely refers to human nature—what we are like at our deepest spiritual, personal, and moral levels. The part of our being that enables us to relate spiritually to God and to one another is what the Bible describes as the image of God.

Dean Nelson, one of the contributors to this chapter, saw an example of this image of God in the experience of a 10-year-old boy from Pasadena. A bigger, older boy at school had been stealing the youngster's lunch. The father of the younger boy responded the way he thought was appropriate—he taught his son methods of self-defense. Soon after the instruction the boy came home buoyant about how the day had gone.

"He didn't take my lunch today, Dad!"

"Which method did you use?" The father said he was imagining his virile son delivering a knockout blow to the bully's chin.

"I didn't use anything you taught me," the boy replied. "I just decided to make him my friend."

After a long pause, the dad said, "Well, that can work too."

This capacity to love and return love is built into the very fabric of life in every man, woman, and child. In some mysterious way, it is what relates us to God.

So when wayward human beings turn to God, they are really coming home to the very foundation of their being. What a powerful thought! Maybe we should mentally stamp on the forehead of every person we meet, "Created in the image of God. Handle with care." Then we might remember that all of us represent an amazing capacity to love and be loved. That is the true nature of God and therefore of us: love.

This is why Jesus had no hesitation in calling us back to loving God with all our hearts and our neighbor as ourselves. Yet this degree of love strikes us as utterly impossible. Our minds are overwhelmed by the suggestion that we should love completely, behave with flawless consistency, and think with nothing but the purest motives. But this capacity seems to have been given to our original parents. And it is to this capacity that we find ourselves being drawn. We have deep within us a yearning to be like our original parents—fully human yet perfect in love toward God and one another.

Being human does not equal being a sinner. If that were so, being human would exclude being morally the way God created and intended us to be. We are human beings in the image of God first, sinners second.

Trouble in Paradise

Even if Adam and Eve behaved like newlyweds, there came a time when the honeymoon was over—their choice, not God's. When someone works for a long time on a college campus, as the writers of this chapter have, they have many opportunities to see couples get married. Many couples begin their relationships in bliss, totally enthralled with each other. Happiness and harmony are the words that best describe their world. It is like the Garden of Eden.

Unfortunately, happiness and harmony can die, making room for anger and discord. Those who once loved can become those who now hate. And those who enjoyed a honeymoon can suffer a divorce. This is also like the Garden of Eden. Eden was the scene of "the great divorce"— the splintering of the love relationship between the Creator and the creatures who had been made for the divine purpose of love.

The Genesis story shows that the root of this divorce was the quest for self-rule. The serpent told Eve that when she ate of the tree of knowledge, "your eyes will be opened, and you will be like God" (Gen. 3:5). She could be the ruler over her own life. This was a powerful temptation. It is the same temptation we struggle with today. But the desire to be ruler over our lives has resulted in disorientation within ourselves and alienation from God, as it did with Adam and Eve.

Theologians often call this desire to rule our own lives, which is present in all humans, "original sin." That's because it reflects the original or first sin in the Garden of Eden. John Wesley, an 18th-century British minister whose emphasis on Holiness made him the theological mentor for the Holiness Movement, said humans were created looking to God for meaning in life. So when we try to rule our own lives we are living contrary to the way God created us. The result is disorientation and confusion.

Throughout the centuries, Christians have struggled to explain how our present human nature is related to Adam and Eve. If original sin is a "thing" that is in our human nature as a result of Adam's sin, then how is it passed from one generation to another? No explanations seem to do a good job answering this question. Augustine, a church leader in the fourth century, said, for example, it was passed on genetically through sex. But God created sex as something good.

It seems best to think of original sin not as a "thing,"

like a disease that can be passed on genetically from generation to generation, but rather as a broken relationship. This broken relationship is seen in our desire to rule our own lives and our alienation from God.

In spite of this alienation, we can cling to the fact that we are made in the image of God. This image is our capacity to love and be loved regardless of circumstances. It is our opportunity to enter completely into loving relationships, in which we are motivated by love rather than by power or selfishness. Though our ability to love has been disrupted by sin, the image of God remains in each of us. And God works through that image to draw us back to the level of relationship with Him and with others that we were created to enjoy.

There is something very good about being human. Our creativity and ingenuity are amazing. But so is our ability to love—an ability that exists because of God's image in us. Yet because the great divorce that took place in Eden gave sin a gateway to humanity, we cannot in our own power live in harmony with God and others. We need help. That help comes from God, who desires that original level of intimacy. He continues to love us and to reach out to us. God recognizes His image in us, perhaps much like we can see ourselves in our children. And because His love never gives up on us, we are able to experience a restored relationship.

What takes place is something similar to what a high school student in Minnesota experienced after getting his father's car stuck in a snowy embankment. The boy had driven onto the expressway late at night after a hockey game, and not until he had been driving for a few moments did he notice headlights coming directly toward him.

He had pulled onto the highway going the wrong way.

Quickly, to get out of the way, he drove onto the median where he promptly got stuck in the snow. A highway patrol officer berated him for his carelessness. The tow truck operator didn't hide his irritation at having to crawl into the snow under the car to attach the chains so the car could be removed.

But neither of those comments bothered the boy as much as what he thought his father would say. He called his father, who was at a dinner party.

"I'll be right over," the dad said. He arrived just as the car was being pulled out of the snowbank and pointed in the right direction.

"Are you OK?" the dad asked.

"Yes."

"Is the car OK?"

"Yes."

The two stood alone in silence in the center of the highway.

"How am I going to get home?" the boy finally asked, handing the keys to his father.

"You're driving," said the dad. "One mistake doesn't mean I stop trusting you. I'll see you later on."

With that the dad returned to his car and drove off.

The boy drove slowly home, exuberant in the confidence his father had placed in him. The boy was his father's son. And in spite of the ditched car, the father could see himself in the boy and loved what he saw.

Our Heavenly Father gave us His own image, and He never stops seeing it in us. *That* is what it really means to be human—to have God see himself in us and provide a way for us to be restored to Him.

In our lifetime we have witnessed that humans are capable of apparently endless creativity and ingenuity. But being human is more than being creative or smart. Being human is living a life in response to God, who made us and saw that His creation was good.

The Short Course

Earning Our Salvation

Even the revered Wesley brothers, John and Charles, had to learn the hard way that it's impossible to find peace with God by doing good deeds. John Wesley, in particular, lived for 15 years in a state of devoted piety—and misery. He eventually learned to trust that God loved him whether or not he fasted every Wednesday and Friday.

Predestined to Be Saved

No individuals are preselected by God for salvation or damnation. Salvation is available for everyone. It is up to us to decide whether or not to accept God's love.

BACKGROUND
SCRIPTURE:
Rom. 6:15-18
Eph. 2:8-9
1 John 4:9-10

Sam Harris
and
Dean Nelson

A Sinning Religion

Though we're saved by God's grace, and not by holy behavior, that's no excuse to take sin lightly. If God's grace is alive and well inside us, we're not going to spend our energy calculating how much sin we can get by with.

2

Grace That Is Greater than All Our Sin

We are not saved by running to God. We are saved by God running to us.

MANY YEARS OF ANTICIPATION and effort had gone into this event—Ron and Susan Wenaas of Minneapolis were finally going to be able to adopt a child. An aircraft from South Korea landed at the Twin Cities International Airport, and the couple paced as they watched the plane pull into the gate. When the passengers unloaded, the Wenaases saw a tiny five-year-old Korean girl among them.

The girl had been prepared by the adoption agency to recognize her new parents. She looked at a picture in her hand, then scanned the crowd and spotted Ron and Susan. She spoke the only two English words she knew.

"Daddy! Mommy!"

The parents had a picture too. Like the little girl, they had been prepared for this meeting. Though the parents and child had never really met, they had already begun the process of knowing each other.

What the adoption agency did for the couple and the little girl is a bit like what God does for all of us in salvation—He prepares the way. Theologians call this prevenient grace, the grace that comes to all people before they meet God in conversion. It's the love God extends to people to show He wants to save everyone.

Some Christians have trouble accepting the idea of grace. They think they have to earn God's love. Even the great hymn writer who helped found Methodism, Charles Wesley, had trouble with the concept.

Charles Wesley was seriously ill when he was visited by Peter Böhler, a missionary and preacher in the Moravian movement—which was known for its emphasis on evangelism and Christian living. During their conversation, Böhler asked Wesley what hope he had for being saved. Wesley replied, "I have done my best to serve God." Böhler said nothing. He just shook his head and left.

Later Wesley reflected, "I thought his response was quite unkind, as though my best efforts were not good enough to hope to be saved. If all that I have done is not enough to be saved, I have nothing else to trust in."

Wesley had reason to be upset. He had been living his life as though his good deeds influenced how God perceived him. For example, in 1729 he organized a small group of Oxford students, nicknamed the Holy Club and later called Methodists, who were devoted to daily Bible study and prayer, visiting the sick, feeding the hungry, and teaching poor children. Later headed by Wesley's older brother, John, the group also fasted each Wednesday and Friday and took Communion weekly. They devoted themselves to strict discipline so that every aspect of their lives would reflect *really outward* inward holiness. Charles even refused a wealthy inheritance so he could become a missionary to the Indians of Georgia.

Wesley eventually came to realize that spiritual success in life could not be measured by the categories of being good or bad. Salvation depends entirely on God's desire to build a relationship with us. The good news is that He decided to love us long before we became either "good people" or "too bad for Him to forgive us." God's grace precedes and actually enables our decision to accept His love for us. This has been a hard concept to grasp, even among Christians. That's because common sense tells us that love is something to be earned.

Temporarily Insecure

John Wesley, the forefather of the Wesleyan Movement, was more than a member of the Holy Club; his disciplined commitment to God would make the most religious among us blush with shame. When he was 22, his father convinced him to become a preacher. At that time Wesley committed himself to being what he called a "good Christian." Each day he prayed for two hours. He tried to keep the whole law of God through careful self-examination and through helping others in need. Yet for all of his devotion and charity, John was miserable. He constantly fought, but never seemed to win, his battle to live a life pleasing to God.

Like his brother Charles, John also served as a missionary to the Georgia Indians. His motive was to glorify God and to save his own soul. But his three-year missionary service turned into a disastrous failure mired in scandal. His worship style proved too formal for the pioneers. And his refusal to give communion to newlyweds John and Sophie Hopkins looked like sour grapes at having lost the battle for Sophie's affection. Wesley wrote in his journal on January 24, 1738, "I went to America to convert the Indians; but O! who shall convert me?"

By 1738 Wesley had lived through some 15 years of frustration over trying to please God—frustration that began when he decided to pursue a career in ministry. Yet we would have to search long and hard to find any greater example of devotion to God. Ironically, it was Wesley's devotion that kept him frustrated. By establishing his own terms for salvation, sincere and devoted though they were, John only intensified his broken relationship with God.

The experience of John and Charles parallels the sin of Adam and Eve. When Adam and Eve disobeyed God, they chose to be self-centered—to do things their own way. Even though they believed in God, they chose to be their own gods, to determine how they would live in this world.

Neither John nor Charles were conscious of any desire to disobey God—quite the opposite—but they were trying to set the terms of their relationship with Him. We can be right with God only when we accept God for who He is—our Creator, Lord, and Savior. We cannot experience a loving relationship with Him if we try to tell Him how He will be our God.

Early in 1738 John Wesley met Peter Böhler. This became a turning point in Wesley's life, for Böhler taught him to rely on God for his salvation—not to rely on his good deeds or on a sense of spiritual achievement. On May 24 of that year, at a Moravian meeting on Aldersgate Street in London, Wesley had a spiritual experience. His journal describes what happened: "I felt my heart strangely warmed. I felt I did trust in Christ, Christ alone for salvation; and an assurance was given to me that he had taken away my sins." Students of history call this Wesley's Aldersgate experience, which marks the point at which Wesley was freed from the anxiety and insecurity that came from trying to be good enough for God. It is when Wesley experienced peace with God.

His struggle reminds us that salvation does not start with ourselves. Without God's prior decision to love us, we would not even care about our relationship with the Lord. But before our misconceptions, before our misguided attempts to find sincerity, before our desire to set our own terms with God, He chose to love us. He refused to let our relationship with Him remain broken. The death and resurrection of Jesus was God's (1) definitive statement that He would never stop loving us, and (2) provision for us to become right with Him again. Because of God's prevenient grace we can be made right with Him through trusting Christ for our hope of salvation.

Are Some Destined to Accept God?

If our salvation depends on God's prior love for us, does that mean everyone will be saved? Some answer by saying God allows only certain people to choose salvation. That is, some are predestined to be saved and others are predestined to be lost. Christians who believe in the doctrine of predestination see support in words such as, "He predestined us to be adopted as his sons through Jesus Christ, in accordance with his pleasure and will" (Eph. 1:5).

People today tend to interpret Scripture solely in terms of the individual. But the writers of Scripture usually considered the individual in terms of the community. In Ephesians 1, Paul was talking not about individuals but about the community. He was describing the way God chose to restore people to a right relationship with himself. God has predestined that all who are saved (and the invitation extends to all people) will be saved by trusting in Christ. God determined how we are to be saved, not *who* will or will not be saved. Our problem is not that God chooses a limited number of people to be saved. Our problem is that, since the sin of Adam and Eve, all of us have been born with a bent toward self-centeredness.

John Wesley said his meeting with Peter Böhler was no accident. God had been working in Wesley's life to prepare him for that meeting. The preparation came in Wesley's childhood training, in 15 frustrating years of not being able to be good enough for God, and in the failed missionary journey. By the time Wesley met with Böhler, God's grace had been working to prepare and enable him to trust solely in God's grace for his salvation.

So even our choice to accept God's grace is a result of God's grace. Because of our sinful tendency to put ourselves at the center of our lives, we would never volunteer to choose to live God's way. But God's grace awakens us and frees us to choose Christ.

Paul put it this way, "Because of his great love for us, God, who is rich in mercy, made us alive with Christ even when we were dead in transgressions—it is by grace you have been saved" (Eph. 2:4-5).

Dead people can't take initiatives. Dead people can't do much of anything. But the living God took the initiative. We don't need to twist His arm to love us. From the very beginning He has loved us, and His grace frees us to choose to love Him.

If We're Saved by Grace Why Not Sin Up a Storm?

If grace reminds us that our hope does not reside in our perfect performance, doesn't this open the door to making sin acceptable among Christians?

Or as Paul put it, "What then? Shall we sin because we are not under law but under grace?" (Rom. 6:15). His reply: "By no means!"

The evidence that we have responded to God's grace is seen in our wholehearted desire that every thought, word, and action should reflect God's love. Grace leaves no room in the heart for calculating how much we can sin and still be Christian.

What about the opposite extreme? If we commit just one sin, does that mean we have lost our salvation? Not if repentance follows. But we must beware of the attitude that excuses sin because of God's grace. If a Christian decides to stop loving God and to return to a life of sinfulness, God won't force that person to be what he or she no longer wants to be. Yet God's grace does not create a neurotic, guilt-ridden piety that is consumed with the fear that

God's love depends on our perfect performance.

Sam Harris, a contributor to this chapter, makes it a habit to regularly tell his daughters that he will always love them and that Jesus will always love them. Rebekah, his oldest daughter, came to him one day and said, "Daddy, even if you stop loving me, I will never stop loving you." He tried to convince her that he would never stop loving her. But she repeated her statement, to which her father repeated that he would never stop loving her. He said he realized later that Bekah wasn't worried that he would stop loving her. She merely wanted to say that her love for him was unconditional.

Unconditional love makes for great relationships. By God's grace we can live in the confidence of His unconditional love for us.

And by God's grace we can live as responsible, obedient people who love God unconditionally.

The Short Course

Inspiration

God did not dictate the Bible. Nor is Scripture merely great literature, the work of inspired geniuses. Throughout history God revealed facts about himself and humanity, then He guided writers to understand the importance of those revelations. The writers used their own language, personality, and historical circumstances to communicate in their own ways the truths God gave them.

Authority

Scripture is the foundational source for Christian beliefs. We can also find direction in the traditions of the church, our powers of reasoning, and personal experiences.

Accuracy

Some Christians hold that the original manuscripts of the books of the Bible had no errors. Problem is, none of the originals seem to have survived. And the question is, what's going to be our attitude toward the Bible we do have—a Bible translated from ancient copies that do include some discrepancies, such as spelling and word order. Of this we can be certain: The truth God wanted to convey is fully and accurately intact.

BACKGROUND
SCRIPTURE:
1 Cor. 1:17-27
2 Tim. 3:16

Dennis Bratcher
and
Dean Nelson

• 30 •

3

How to Use,
and Not Abuse,
the Bible

*If you read it in the Word, but it seems
unreasonable, doesn't track with what you've
seen of life, and wouldn't fly at church, you
probably read it wrong.*

ELLEN THOUGHT that all she needed to know for the day was in the "promise box" she kept by her bedside. When there were tough times at work, a promise from the box kept her going. If she was facing a difficult decision, the promise box gave her hope and direction.

Even when her husband, Jim, first got sick, Ellen knew God would heal him; a card from the promise box told her so. Her faith never wavered even as Jim grew worse.

When an ambulance took Jim to the hospital, Ellen paused long enough to call someone in her church's prayer chain. She was still confident God would work a miracle. As she sat in the hospital chapel, she prayed and opened her Bible to the Book of Exodus where she found these words in 15:26: "If you will diligently hearken to the voice of the LORD your God, and do that which is right in his eyes, give heed to his commandments and keep all his statutes, I will put none of the diseases upon you which I put upon the

Egyptians; for I am the LORD, your healer" (RSV).

This was her answer, she believed. God would heal Jim. He said so right there in His Word.

A few hours later Jim died. Ellen was devastated. She believed God had failed her, and both the Bible and the promise box were full of lies.

The problem, however, was not really with God or the Bible. The problem was with Ellen's use of the Bible. She had built a set of beliefs based on a collection of unrelated verses. She used her Bible, but her conclusions were not necessarily biblical. It had never dawned on her that some of what she believed might have been different from the intended message of the Bible.

With the help of family and friends, Ellen took a closer look at Scripture and rebuilt her faith in God and His Word. But there are plenty of other Ellens out there: people who develop their entire set of beliefs through an incomplete use of the Bible.

How to Abuse the Bible

Ellen was not wrong in believing God could heal her husband. She was not wrong in believing that the Bible contains promises for us to claim. Where Ellen strayed was in making the Bible something it is not: a fortune cookie. Crack it open and there, somewhere in the middle, is always a message just for you. God sometimes does speak to us in this way. Many of us can testify to this kind of experience. However, the danger of this approach is that it can lead us to read more into the biblical text than is there.

There's a variation of this belief that Christians sometimes use to oppress people who don't agree with them. It's the belief that the Bible magically holds the specific answer to every possible question humans face. All we have to do is figure out how to break the Bible's code so that we can discover God's hidden message.

Earlier Christians, for example, used their creative interpretations of isolated Bible passages to condemn people who said the earth was not the center of the universe. And it's not that long ago that some used the Bible to argue that God himself had decided African people should be slaves.

People still take scripture out of context, to manipulate God into saying what they want to hear. That's what Ellen did, though she did it unknowingly.

Others go to the opposite extreme. They aren't guilty of taking the Bible too far, they don't take the Bible at all. They prefer a scientific approach to life—one that has little room for God. They can accept the Bible and the doctrines of the church as long as the teachings make sense and correspond to evidence they can verify. But when the Bible or creeds start talking about spiritual matters, such as life after death, they are rejected as fantasy, wishful thinking, or superstition.

Fortunately, these two extremes are not the only options.

John Wesley's Tips on What to Believe

John Wesley, the 18th-century forefather of the Wesleyan Movement, understood how hard it can be to decide what to believe and what not to believe.

He identified four interrelated tools that can help us decide what to believe and how to live as Christians. Scholars call his idea the Wesleyan Quadrilateral. He said our Christian faith should be based on:

1. The Bible. It is the undisputed, foundational source of our doctrines and beliefs.

2. Tradition. Wesley knew that people don't read the Bible in a vacuum. They are—and should be—influenced by traditions and interpretations of other Christians throughout the ages.

3. Reason. Wesley's study of Scripture and the early traditions of the Church convinced him that God had created the human intellect as part of His good creation. He also understood that God could and does redeem the entire human person, including the intellect.

So Wesley came to the conclusion that human reason, enabled by the Holy Spirit, plays an important role in helping us understand the Bible and the Christian faith.

4. *Experience.* As Wesley watched God at work in the lives of coal miners in the Welsh revival, he came to understand that unless a belief can be lived out, it probably does not reflect authentic Christian teaching. If the teaching seems Christian, but is impossible to practice, it's not Christian.

Let's take a closer look at each of these.

1. We confess the Bible is God's Word. The Bible is more than a collection of human stories, laws, and folklore. Through its messages, God speaks to us and shows us how He has revealed himself through human history. As Protestants we affirm, as Martin Luther did during the 16th-century Reformation, the Bible is our only reliable source of understanding about God and how He relates to His creation.

As the statement of faith of one Holiness denomination says, Scripture contains "all truth necessary to faith and Christian living."[1]

We can't stop there, however. We need to do more than accept it as God's Word. As Ellen's case vividly illustrates, we should learn to understand it.

It's at this point—interpreting the Scripture—that Christians begin to disagree. There's a lot of debate, for example, over the issue of inspiration. One of the key questions is this: To what extent was God involved in producing the Bible?

Actually, this debate grows more from basic assumptions about the nature of human beings than from an examination of the Bible.

Position 1: God Wrote It. Some say God virtually wrote

the Bible himself. A few say God went so far as to dictate to the author the very words to write, sometimes without the writer understanding anything he wrote.

A more moderate and more widely held variation of this position is that God revealed the message to individuals but sometimes allowed the writer to choose his own words and style of expression.

In both approaches, the human author acts only as the muscle and bone for God's writing; God is solely responsible for the content.

Usually underlying this view is the belief that human beings have been totally and irredeemably corrupted by sin. As sinful human beings, the writers were considered incapable of understanding enough about God to write Scripture. If humans were involved, the message was corrupted. This is the classic Augustinian-Calvinistic position of human incapability. It springs from the teachings of Augustine (A.D. 354-430) and John Calvin (1509-64) and shows up in many Baptist, Presbyterian, and independent churches.

A logical extension of this position is the idea of inerrancy—that the Bible has no mistakes of any kind. As the argument goes, if God is responsible for all the content and even the very words of the Bible, then there can be no errors at all—not in theology, history, science, or any other area. In this view, whenever the Bible refers to any fact in any area, it must be totally accurate in all details.

Since there are some discrepancies in the earliest existing manuscripts (spelling, for example), some hold that only the first copies of the Bible as originally written by the first authors were entirely without error. Unfortunately, none of these original manuscripts exists today. What we do have are modern translations based on the earliest copies available.

Position 2: Humans Wrote It. On the flip side of the issue, some believe the inspiration is mostly from human genius, as in any great work of literature.

The Bible is good writing and expresses valuable insights about human beings in the world. But the inspiration comes, at least to a large degree, from within the writer. Some who take this position, however, would acknowledge God's involvement in at least part of the process.

If this position is accurate, then the Bible would stand as a tribute to its writers as the works of John Bunyan or C. S. Lewis have become monuments of their elevated thoughts.

Position 3: God Inspired People to Write It. There's a position between these two extremes. Some Christians say God inspired people to understand His revelation, while entrusting them with an important role in producing Scripture.

This view is called the plenary theory of inspiration. It's the position taken by many Holiness denominations. The word *plenary* means "full"; this emphasizes that Bible truths are fully reliable because they have come from God. They are indeed "God's Word."

The belief here is that God divinely revealed himself in history (scholars call this revelation) and then helped the writers of Scripture understand (inspiration) the importance of that revelation. The writers then used their own language, personality, and historical circumstances to communicate in their own ways the truths that God had helped them understand about himself.

This is the reason it is so important for students of the Word to discover, as much as possible, the context in which a particular passage was written. By examining the situation impacting a biblical writer, we can see more clearly the writer's intended message. Using tools—like Bible dictionaries and encyclopedias, maps, commentaries, and even various translations or versions of the Bible—provides added understanding.

Behind these views of plenary inspiration is the conviction that human beings, although sinful, have *not* been irreparably and irredeemably corrupted by sin. Through God's grace and forgiveness and the working of the Holy Spirit, we can be totally reoriented toward God. People are capable of genuine change. Through the presence of God's Holy Spirit, human beings can understand and witness to truths about God.

This conviction is the Wesleyan-Arminian understanding of God's enabling grace. It grows out of the teachings of John Wesley (1703-91) and Jacobus Arminius (1560-1609).

From the Wesleyan perspective, the Bible communicates three things. It tells us:

about the nature and character of God;

about the nature and character of human beings;

how to respond to God.

This message comes in a great variety of ways: with different types of literature, from different periods of history, through different people speaking different languages, using different styles of writing, and emphasizing different themes. But in the middle of all this diversity is unity, for the message is directed at these three areas.

This understanding implies some things the Bible is not.

Though the Bible speaks about our physical world, it is not meant to be a detailed, scientific textbook about the physical properties of the universe. And though the Bible deals with God's revelation throughout human history, it is not meant to be a history book intended to provide us with a complete documentary of the ancient world. In addition, though the Bible gives us a glimpse of the future, it does not offer a detailed account. Nor is it intended to provide us with coded messages that answer every question we can imagine.

The people who wrote the Bible most likely believed the earth was flat and the sun revolved around the earth. These were common misconceptions in ancient times.

They probably had no idea what a dinosaur was or that a fault line in the earth's crust can generate an earthquake. They were ordinary people of faith who lived with a limited view of the physical world. Yet they wrote extraordinary things about God as He revealed himself to them.

We believe that when they tell us about God, about ourselves, and about how we should relate to God, they are speaking God's truth. In this respect, Wesleyan Holiness people can strongly state that the Bible is "the trustworthy record of God's revelation, completely truthful in all it affirms. It has been faithfully preserved and proves itself true in human experience."[2]

2. In attempting to understand the Bible, we operate within a tradition that gives us guidelines about how to interpret Scripture. We modern-day Protestants are sometimes suspicious of tradition, and we complain it can inhibit more than contribute.

"We've never done it that way before" can bring on inflexibility, stagnation, and slow death. On the other hand, there may be a good reason "We've never done it that way before." In some areas of our life, we need change. But in others we need stability. Tradition provides that.

Christian traditions refer to ideas and beliefs about God, salvation, and other spiritual matters that the Christian community has passed down through the centuries. Different religious groups share many of the same traditions but have also developed distinct traditions. For instance, Wesleyan-Arminian churches have traditionally emphasized that humans need reconciliation with God and each other, that the grace of God makes such reconciliation possible, and that it is up to us to respond to God's grace. There are other churches that have traditionally taught it is not up to us to decide—God decides who will and will not respond.

These traditions are not essential for determining our

salvation (there will be Wesleyans and Calvinists in heaven). But they do give us a frame of reference for interpreting Scripture and for deciding what to believe and how to behave. And as we saw in Ellen's case, we act on what we believe.

If we do not let our tradition and heritage speak to us, if we cut ourselves off from the insights gained by other Christians worshiping God across the centuries, we risk preventing God from strengthening and guiding us through others who have fought the same battles we are fighting.

Rather than being a demanding taskmaster, our tradition can become a gentle shepherd leading us to new insights into Scripture and new depths of Christian maturity.

3. Wesleyans have a high opinion of human intellect. The reason is the emphasis John Wesley put on God's grace. This grace enables sinful human beings to respond to God, making them "new creations" in Christ. The genuine change allows people to be in harmony with God's purpose and to use their God-given intellects to serve Him.

In some corners of the Holiness church there are people suspicious of any intellectual aspect of the faith. They seem to fear that "thinking" is the opposite of "being spiritual" and that "reason" is the opposite of "faith."

Paul did warn of people who thought they were wise but were actually foolish. He warned about "empty philosophies" that prevent people from believing in a God who would come to earth and die on a cross—it just didn't make sense to them (1 Cor. 1:17-27). It is possible to become so logical and to depend so entirely on rational understanding that we lose the sense of mystery and awe of God and His work.

Often, however, Wesleyans who fear reason or intellect do so because they've been influenced by the pessimistic views of humanity that prevail in other traditions.

For example, some churches teach there is very little in Christianity that we feeble-minded humans can understand. It is all mystery, and we should simply accept it, not questioning anything.

In churches like these, people focus on emotion. Feelings become the ultimate and perhaps only proof God is real and dwells among them. They don't have access to the other evidences that surface when Christians candidly discuss penetrating questions.

These views sell God short, not to mention the human beings He created.

By recognizing the grace of God at work with our own humanity, we can better appreciate how reason can help us understand what we should believe and how we should live as Christians. Mature, Christian understanding comes through effort, struggle, study, and thought, all worked out in the experiences of day-to-day living, and all submitted to God with the prayer, "Lord, help me understand."

The Wesleyan tradition affirms that, while our salvation is appropriated by *faith*, through God's enabling, we can *understand* some things.

4. One of John Wesley's greatest contributions to the Christian faith was his insistence that genuine Christian beliefs could be lived out in real-life experience.

There were two guidelines he followed here.

The first comes from Paul's letter to the Corinthians (1 Corinthians 12—14). For a religious experience to be a valid source of truth about God, it must be for the good of the entire community of faith. If it hurts the community, don't trust it as a source of truth.

Though people may have individual religious experiences, such as visions or bursts of insight they believe come from God, these should not be used as the basis for a belief or practice unless they strengthen the entire community. Personal religious experiences that produce division in the church should be questioned and evaluated against the Word of God.

Wesley's second guideline was that the experience must be in line with Scripture, with the tradition of the community, and be confirmed by reason. If, for example, a Christian friend of yours says God told him to do something you know is contrary to Scripture, against the standard procedures of the church, and doesn't make a bit of sense, don't ask to join him.

Any truth we discover about God through our experience must be supported by the other means of arriving at religious truth. And the opposite is true too. What we Wesleyans believe about God, our sinfulness, grace, redemption, and sanctification is valid only if we can live it out in all aspects of our lives. When we are "walking in the Spirit," we will have a communion with God that will encompass the message in Scripture, passed on by tradition, and confirmed by reason.

If we allow the Bible to come alive within us, if we hear its message echoing through the traditions of our community, if we think and work at understanding its truths, if we allow the truths to become evident in our daily living, we can open up a new window to God. Through it the fresh breezes of the Spirit can begin to animate our understanding in ways we have not imagined. Deeper insight and truths seen in new ways can become the source of new vigor in our walk with God.

And we will not be the same again.

---

1. *Manual,* Church of the Nazarene, 1993-97 ed. (Kansas City: Nazarene Publishing House), par. 26.2, p. 35.

2. *Book of Discipline,* Free Methodist Church of North America, 1989 ed., par. A-108, p. 10.

The Short Course

God Is Holy

God is without anything that even hints of evil.

Humans Can't Fully Understand Him

How can finite, natural beings hope to understand fully an infinite, supernatural God? Operating from this side of eternity, we have no frame of reference to understand some aspects of God—such as the Trinity.

He Is Personal

It's amazing that human beings can develop a personal relationship with the Creator of the universe.

He Is Always Near

Even when we can't sense Him or recognize His work among us, He is here.

He's One God, Three Persons

BACKGROUND
SCRIPTURE:
Deut. 6:4
Job 38
Ps. 145:8-9, 18-21

**Howard Culbertson
and
Dean Nelson**

Even biblical scholars who have been studying the Bible all their lives can't fully explain the concept of the Trinity. But it's in the Bible. "The Lord is one" (Deut. 6:4). "I and the Father are one" (John 10:30). "Make disciples of all nations, baptizing them in the name of the Father and of the Son and of the Holy Spirit" (Matt. 28:19).

4

What God Is Like

If humans could understand God, He wouldn't be God. But He has revealed enough of himself to assure us He is worthy of our trust and our love.

GODS come in all shapes and sizes. People worship big gods and small gods, gods with stunning beauty and gods who have multiple arms, legs, warts, and tongues.

There are gods who live nearby and gods who live far away. There are bloody-clawed gods who enjoy eating human flesh. And there are smiling gods who bend a friendly ear to anyone.

What about our Creator, the one true God who has revealed himself in Scripture? What is He like?

You won't find in the Bible an essay that zeros in on the theme: "The Nature of God." Even Jesus, when He told parables of what the kingdom of God is like, rarely said what *God* is like. Though we won't find in the Bible a definitive description of God, we can find examples of how He interacts with human beings. And through these accounts we have access to deep insights about Him.

When you think about it, it's amazing that human beings can know God in the personal way that we do—that we can develop a personal relationship with the Creator of the universe. No wonder the Psalmist asked, "What is man that you are mindful of him . . . ?" (Ps. 8:4). Still, the testimony of God's people through the ages is that God *is* mindful of us and has provided a way for us to get to know Him in a very personal way.

Our Creator God is much more than some impersonal force of the universe that we can harness with our mental powers. The experience of humanity, recorded both in Scripture and in Christian writings, has shown that God loves us and expresses compassion in personal ways that no mere creative force could do. This personal God gives us glimpses of himself through the lives of His people—in the Bible and in modern times too.

Alexandra Marcus works for a compassionate ministry organization in southern Africa, where she coordinates assistance programs for refugees. In an interview with a documentary film crew, she told of recoiling from the scenes of pillage, rape, deprivation, and starvation. She said she marveled at how the refugees who were Christians held onto their trust in God.

One of the women she talked to had suffered "atrocities that I find very difficult to verbalize." Still, the woman had a vibrant Christian testimony. Her radiant countenance caused the emotional Marcus to ask: "With all this happening around you, how can you believe in God?"

"My God is not doing this," the lady said. "Man is doing this. My Bible tells me God loves me."

"But, tangibly," asked Marcus, "how can you be sure that God loves you?"

"Because you came. You brought me His love," the woman responded.

The same God who brought Marcus and her organization's resources to this woman is the One who brought life-sustaining ravens to Elijah and life-changing love to His human creation.

Warped Notions About God

Most Christians agree that God is a personal God.

That's because most of us have experienced a personal encounter with Him, a time or times in which we have become aware of His personal presence or help.

Beyond that common ground, however, we begin to part company. As a result, there are some very inadequate notions about Him floating around out there.

Pouncer. One is that God is waiting to pounce on us whenever we step out of line. When preachers have talked about "the all-seeing eye of God," they may have given the impression that God is spying on us through a little hole in the ceiling.

A famous preacher of Colonial times, Jonathan Edwards, came from a background that made the sovereignty, or authority, of God the central focus of theology. And on July 8, 1741, he expressed this by preaching a sermon that became a classic—perhaps the most famous sermon in American history: "Sinners in the Hands of an Angry God."

Addressing the sinners in a church at Enfield, Conn., he said, "The God that holds you over the pit of hell, much as one holds a spider, or some loathsome insect, over the fire, abhors you, and is dreadfully provoked: his wrath towards you burns like fire; he looks upon you as worthy of nothing else, but to be cast in the fire; he is of purer eyes than to bear to have you in his sight; you are ten thousand times more abominable in his eyes, than the most hateful venomous serpent is in ours."

That's just a short excerpt of the sermon that eyewitness Stephen Williams wrote in his diary. He said the sermon created "a great moaning and crying out through ye whole House." If you read the sermon in its entirety, you come away with the impression that God is indeed waiting to pounce on us and perhaps even takes fiendish delight in doing it.

Pushover. At the opposite end of the spectrum are

those who think of God as an easy touch. He's got even a softer heart than Santa Claus because though He knows who's naughty and nice, He's going to give everybody the big present: eternal life in heaven.

People with this image of God ask, "How could a loving God send people to hell?" Their answer is a resounding, "He won't. God is love, and love always forgives."

Sugardaddy. A variation of the "Pushover God" is the God who has everything and who wants His Kingdom Kids to have everything too.

The creed of these Christians is, "You do not have, because you do not ask" (James 4:2).

Stephen Miller, editorial committee member, once worked with a Christian who said he believed in this kind of a God. "God is a King," he once told Miller, "and He wants us to have the best of everything." The believer went on to tell about his spiritual victory over going to the self-service island at the gas station. "It's cheaper to go to self-service, but I knew God wanted me to have full-service." Miller said it apparently never occurred to the man that he could get self-service gasoline and use the savings to help someone else—like a starving woman in South Africa, or in south Kansas City for that matter.

People who believe in what is called the "health and wealth gospel" take scriptures out of context and turn biblical teachings upside down. For James also says, "When you ask, you do not receive, because you ask with wrong motives, that you may spend what you get on your pleasures" (4:3). As the Westminster Catechism puts it, humanity's chief end is to glorify God. It's not the other way around. The Psalmist and the apostle Paul would agree (Ps. 86:12; Rom. 15:6).

Why do these warped notions survive? Frankly, it's partly because Christian theologians tend not to speak English. At least not everyday English. They are so concerned about being theologically precise that they use technical words that mean little or nothing to people who don't lunch in the library.

Among their favorites are what we could call the "omnis." Omnipotent, omniscient, and omnipresent, which say God is all-powerful, all-knowing, and always present. Other terms theologians often use are even less comprehensible to laypersons, which makes God less comprehensible: immutable, immense, eternal, almighty, most absolute.

Terms like these leave us with the impression that God is harsh, cold, distant, and indifferent. Part of our problem is that language alone cannot adequately convey the full picture of the Creator who, while in the act of creating, pitches His tent among His creation.

What God Is Really Like

Here's some good advice for getting past the warped teachings and stilted Christian jargon. It comes from J. Kenneth Grider, now retired professor of theology at Nazarene Theological Seminary. Writing in *Basic Christian Doctrines,* he said, "Off with our shoes, for [this] is holy ground . . . Here, logic and mathematics do not suffice. The need is rather for a listening ear, an obedient heart, rapt adoration, a careful engagement with the Holy Scriptures."

In the end, some aspects of God cannot be proved or explained by human logic. But we know them to be true because of His revelation through Scripture and through our experiences with Him. And when we wish to know more, and to understand that which human beings on this side of eternity cannot possibly grasp, He reminds us as He reminded an inquiring and complaining Job. "Where were you when I laid the earth's foundations? . . . Who watched over the birth of the sea . . . ? . . . Have you ever seen the door-keepers of the place of darkness? . . . Have you visited the storehouse of the snow or seen the arsenal where hail is stored . . . ? . . . Who put wisdom in depths of darkness and veiled understanding in secrecy?" (Job 38:4, 8, 17, 22, 36, NEB).

Job's response is the only one possible, given the depths of the unknown that have just been presented to him: "I put my hand over my mouth" (Job 40:4).

Though there is much we cannot know about God, there are some important facts we can know.

He Is Holy. One theme about God running through all of Scripture is that He is holy. *Holiness* is a hard term to understand, but it sums up all of God's perfection. It goes beyond moral behavior and says that God possesses all goodness; He is without anything that even suggests evil.

This is a primary theme to gaining some understanding of God.

He Is Beyond Understanding. God is more than we can grasp, as illustrated in the passage from Job 38. He is not just confusing or hard to conceptualize. God is beyond human understanding.

Our inability to totally explain or define God should reassure us rather than frustrate us. After all, if we completely understood God, He wouldn't be God. How can the natural hope to understand the supernatural, or the finite to understand the Infinite?

Though He made us in His image, He is more than a superversion of humanity. There is an awesome otherness about God. He is the supreme power in the universe, the source of all other existence.

He Is Always Near. *Omnipresent* seems too cold a word to describe God's "immanence," His presence in the world and within us. This concept of God may be one of the most difficult to believe. Sadly, we don't often sense His presence in our lives or notice Him at work in the history of the planet.

But He *is* at work within us and around us.

When there was no organized Christian church in the former Soviet Union or in Communist China, God was there. And when the Berlin wall came down and as the bamboo curtain slowly started to rise, we began to discover Christians by the thousands.

God is not limited to traditional methods of working out His will in our world or in our lives. He still uses Scripture, worship services, and private devotions. But He also uses uncommon means, such as visions, near-death experiences, and acts of nature. He can even work His will through denominations that have mistaken doctrines; or even through world leaders who have no relationship with Him.

He Is One God, Three Persons. People of other faiths accuse Christians of worshiping three gods.

Some correctly point out that the word *Trinity* doesn't appear in Scripture. The concept, however, does. And it's a tough concept to wade through. However, it was not one from which the Early Church shrank. The pronouncements of those early councils are clear and unequivocal, each one building on the other and responding to heretical views about the Godhead.

The fact is, even theologians don't understand the idea of the Trinity very well. It's another one of the mysteries of God that we acknowledge rather than fully understand.

We acknowledge that there is one God in three persons. The Bible doesn't explain how this could be, but it does state this as fact:

There is one God. "Hear, O Israel: The LORD our God, the LORD is one" (Deut. 6:4).

The Son is God. "My Lord and my God!" Thomas said to Jesus (John 20:28). "I and the Father are one," Jesus said (10:30). Paul refers to "Christ, who is God over all" (Rom. 9:5).

The Holy Spirit is God. Several times in Scripture the Father, Son, and Holy Spirit are named together in a coordinate way. During the ritual of baptism many Christians use Jesus' statement from Matt. 28:19, "In the name of the Father and of the Son and of the Holy Spirit." Paul, in 1 Cor. 3:16-17 and 6:19, equates the Holy Spirit with God residing within us.

The word *Trinity* does not appear in Scripture. But the concept is a combination of these biblical truths: There is but one God; the Father, the Son, and the Holy Spirit are all referred to as God. All three are personally distinct from one another, distinguished by personal pronouns, but working in unison to accomplish the continuous task of creative love and reconciliation.

Though we may not fully grasp this concept, the Trinity helps us gain a clearer picture of how God is not remote or far away, of how salvation has come to us, and of how God's continuous presence guides us in holy living.

He Is Love. The statement "God is love" comes from 1 John 4:8. It means more than: God shows us love, or God has love, or even that God loves. To say "God is love" is to say something about His very essence. The most memorized verse of the Bible may well be John 3:16. That verse, which even appears on placards at major sporting events, says something fundamental about who and what God is.

God loved the world so much that He sent His only Son to save us. God is a missionary God. This God of redeeming love and power is One who seeks to make all people His sons and daughters (John 1:12-13). He is not so much a gift-giver as He is a seeker of lost sheep. This is a far cry from some people's image of a God who wants to satisfy all our desires, including the selfish ones.

One evening as family devotions were concluding in the Howard Culbertson home, one of the parents prayed, "Thank You, Heavenly Father, for Your presence."

Immediately after the "amen," four-year-old Rachel said, "Presents? Where are the presents?"

That's what many Christians today expect of God. Presents. But what He gives us instead expresses so much better His loving nature that seeks to transform and redeem us. For He gives us His presence.

The Short Course

Jesus Is Unique

He sets Christianity apart from other religions that worship only one God. Other faiths don't worship Jesus as God or consider Him worthy of saying, "I am the way and the truth and the life. No one comes to the Father except through me" (John 14:6).

He Was God and Man

Christians have long debated just how human Jesus really was, and how divine. Some have said He was a human whom God adopted at the Jordan River baptism. Others said He was God who only appeared human. But without understanding how it is possible, most Christians have settled on the belief that Jesus was fully divine and fully human. "I and the Father are one" (John 10:30). "The Word became flesh and made his dwelling among us" (1:14).

His Death and Resurrection

BACKGROUND
SCRIPTURE:
Mark 10:45
John 1:1, 14; 14:6-11
Heb. 4:15
1 John 4:2-3, 10

Jirair Tashjian
and
Dean Nelson

Christ's crucifixion and resurrection not only give us hope in life after death but also give us the motivation and power to break free of our enslavement to sin in this lifetime. "Our old self was crucified with him so that the body of sin might be done away with, that we should no longer be slaves to sin . . . count yourselves dead to sin but alive to God in Christ Jesus" (Rom. 6:6, 11).

5

It's Jesus Who Makes Christianity Unique

Like Jews and Muslims, Christians are the people of one God and one Book. But they part company when Jesus says, "I am the way and the truth and the life. No one comes to the Father except through me" (John 14:6).

JEWS WORSHIP ONE GOD. So do Muslims. So do Christians. The great religions of the world have many things in common. But there is something that sets them apart from each other.

The uniqueness of the Christian faith in large part lies in our belief that God has come to us in the person of Jesus Christ, the God-Man.

In Islam, Muhammad is considered the greatest of prophets—greater even than Jesus, whom they also consider a prophet. But they don't think of Muhammad as divine. To do so would be blasphemy.

Buddhism, however, is another story. Buddha, his proponents say, managed to transcend human limitations and attain enlightenment, which is similar to divine status. But that enlightenment is also possible for anyone who seriously pursues Buddhism. In this sense, Buddha is not unique. He has only attained what others can also attain.

In Christianity, though, Jesus was uniquely God on

earth, in the form of a human being.

How could that possibly be? How could an infinite God be, at the same time, a finite human being? How could Jesus be both the eternal Word of God and, as we read in John 1:1 and 14, the Word that became flesh?

When Christian theologians say Jesus is the "God-Man" they do not mean He is half God and half man. Nor do they mean He is God and only appeared to be human when He came to earth. Rather, He was really and truly human, and really and truly divine, 100 percent each. It is in the historical, human person of Jesus that God comes to be Immanuel, a word meaning "God with us" (Matt. 1:23).

Confused About Jesus

In the first few centuries of Christianity, some Christian groups tried to simplify the matter about what kind of entity Jesus was.

Some, primarily Jewish Christians, tried to resolve the paradox by emphasizing the humanity of Jesus. Because of their Jewish background, they were familiar with what is called the Shema (sha-MAH)—which became the creed for the Jewish faith: "Hear, O Israel: The LORD our God, the LORD is one" (Deut. 6:4). Because they had understood that God is one, they could not see how Jesus could be divine. As far as they were concerned, to say that Jesus was God was to contradict the Old Testament affirmation that God is one.

So they taught that Jesus was the adopted Son of God, not fully divine as God is. The adoption took place when the voice from heaven came at Jesus' baptism, proclaiming, "You are my Son, whom I love; with you I am well pleased" (Mark 1:11). Most Christians eventually rejected this view. Instead, the church chose to live with the mystery of the God-Man paradox rather than opt for an inadequate simplification.

Another group tried to resolve the problem by arguing that Jesus Christ was truly God, but He only appeared to be human. In this view, Jesus was a spirit disguised as a person with a human body. He had all power and knowledge but chose not to reveal them, except in a limited way, in order to accommodate himself to the society and the culture of His time. Again, the New Testament writers, as well as the Early Church, rejected this explanation and chose to stay with the God-Man paradox.

Apparently 1 John was written partly to combat this notion that Jesus only appeared human. For John wrote, "By this you know the Spirit of God: every spirit that confesses that Jesus Christ has come in the flesh is from God, and every spirit that does not confess Jesus is not from God" (4:2-3, NRSV).

The Gospel of John also declares, "In the beginning was the Word, and the Word was with God, and the Word was God" (1:1). A little later we read, "The Word became flesh and made his dwelling among us" (v. 14).

This is where we see Immanuel explained—God is with us in human flesh. Theologians use *incarnation* to describe this event because the word means to become flesh. Jesus, then, is the incarnation of God.

If we abandon the divine nature of Jesus, we end up rejecting the idea that God has come to us in the person of Jesus Christ. And if God has not come to us in Christ, He remains remote and we cannot know Him in a personal and intimate way.

On the other hand, if we abandon the humanity of Jesus, we deny the incarnation. When we make Jesus all divine but not human, He would be far removed from where we live—far from our trials and temptations, far from our pain and suffering, far from our finite existence. We could even excuse our sinfulness by saying that the reason Jesus was able to live a holy life was because He was God. We might ask, How can I be holy when I'm only human? But Heb. 4:15 reminds us, "We do not have a high priest who is unable to sympathize with our weaknesses, but we have one who has been tempted in every way, just as we are— yet was without sin."

Jesus got tired, thirsty, and hungry. The Gospel of John, especially, emphasizes that Jesus was subject to the normal limitations and emotions of the human body. He was overcome by sorrow and wept at the tomb of Lazarus. He enjoyed eating with friends and acquaintances so much that He was accused wrongly of being a glutton. He experienced anger. Though a miracle-worker, He was bound by time and space. He lived at a particular time in history and lived according to the customs of the day. Even historians, such as Josephus of first-century Palestine, confirm that Jesus lived then and there.

Though Jesus spoke more about the kingdom of God than about himself, He did speak clearly about who He is.

In John, Jesus makes several "I am" statements: "I am the way and the truth and the life. No one comes to the Father except through me" (14:6). "Anyone who has seen me has seen the Father" (v. 9). "I and the Father are one" (10:30).

And in Luke we read of Him saying, "All things have been committed to me by my Father. No one knows who the Son is except the Father, and no one knows who the Father is except the Son and those to whom the Son chooses to reveal him" (10:22).

When Jesus was asked during His trial if He was the Messiah, He said, "I am," and then quoted Dan. 7:13, which portrays the Son of Man at the right hand of God and coming with the clouds of heaven.

One reason there were so many debates in the Early Church over Christ's divine and human nature is that the New Testament had no clear-cut statement on the subject.

So the Church had to figure out a way to express this essential truth about Jesus. Over the first several centuries various Christians tried. But it wasn't until A.D. 325 that the truth was expressed in what became known as the Nicene Creed. In part, the creed explains that Christ is the "true God of true God, begotten not made, of one substance with the Father."

Why Jesus Died

Paul says, "Christ died for our sins according to the Scriptures, . . . he was buried, . . . he was raised on the third day" (1 Cor. 15:3-4). Mark quotes Jesus as saying, "The Son of Man did not come to be served, but to serve, and to give his life as a ransom for many" (10:45).

Yet, He prayed in Gethsemane, "Take this cup from me" (Mark 14:36). If He believed that His death was essential for our salvation, why would He ask God to let Him please skip it?

In fact, if Jesus was God, why did He pray at all? Wouldn't that be like talking to himself? Let's tackle this question first.

Prayer is communion, communication, and expression of love between human beings and God. Christianity presents God as three persons in one—Father, Son, and Holy Spirit. When Jesus prayed, He lovingly and willingly submitted himself to the will of the Father—showing that the Son depended on the Father for everything. Jesus, as second person of the Trinity, was in perfect harmony and union with the Father.

In addition, we should remember that Jesus, as the incarnate Son of God, was aware of His finite existence and limitations as human and His need for God's presence and provision made available through prayer.

On the subject of why He prayed to escape death, the Gospels record that Jesus went to Jerusalem to proclaim

His message of the kingdom of God. He knew that Jerusalem was a dangerous place to do such a thing. He was quite aware of the political and religious climate in the city. The Temple—the center of religious authority —was there. But the Romans were also garrisoned there. They would act swiftly and harshly against any public show of Jewish nationalism. The Romans as well as the Jewish leaders could easily interpret that the kingdom of God proclaimed by Jesus was a threat to the social, political, and religious institutions. Yet Jesus felt compelled to preach in Jerusalem what He had been preaching in Galilee, in spite of the risks. He was committed to carrying out the demands of the kingdom of God in Jerusalem even if it meant His own death. But His prayer in Gethsemane shows He had no desire to suffer the Crucifixion, if there was another way to accomplish God's will. But there wasn't.

Jesus died in an agonizing and humiliating way, crying out, "My God, my God, why have you forsaken me?" (Mark 15:34). These words are from Ps. 22:1. It's not that God abandoned Jesus, nor that Jesus doubted God in His dying moments. Rather, Jesus was turning to God and quoting scripture during the darkest moments of His life. Psalm 22 is for just such a time. But it's a passage, too, that ends on a note of praise for the Lord and perhaps with a subtle reference to the impact the Crucifixion would have on the world: "Future generations will be told about the Lord. They will proclaim his righteousness to a people yet unborn" (vv. 30-31).

Jesus did not die hopelessly or in bitter disillusionment. He died believing that His death was not going to be in vain, that this was not the end. Jesus died believing that His death was the only way the kingdom of God could come.

He was not mistaken. The kingdom of God did come, for God raised His Son from death and through Jesus offered the hope of salvation to the whole world.

Why the Resurrection of Jesus Is So Important

Perhaps the most important thing the New Testament says about the Resurrection is that Jesus was raised by God the Father. This means the Resurrection was something God himself did. It didn't just happen; Jesus didn't just arise. It was God who reversed death itself.

After everything that sinful humanity had done to extinguish the life of Jesus, God acted in a mighty show of His power. He raised His Son and through Him offered grace and salvation to all of us. It is for this reason that Christ's death is redemptive for us. His death and resurrection are a demonstration of God's love and grace for us. As 1 John 4:10 says, "This is love: not that we loved God, but that he loved us and sent his Son as an atoning sacrifice for our sins."

There are plenty of theories that suggest God had no part in the Resurrection. One says His body was only resuscitated after the trauma of the Crucifixion, much like some people today are discovered still alive when they are delivered to the morgue or the mortician. Christ's resurrection was nothing like that. It was a dramatic demonstration that God has power even over death, and that the end of life on earth is not the end of life.

The Resurrection, also, is a provision to empower us to stop living a life of sin.

Reuben Welch, evangelist, author, and college professor, said in a recent outdoor Easter service in San Diego, "The story of Jesus dying and God raising Him from the dead is not just a tragic story that has a happy ending. It is a story that shows how God provided a way for the human race to break out of its cycle of sinning."

The human race was in a downward spiral of sin, Welch explained. Jesus' resurrection broke the spiral and provided a way for individuals to begin an upward spiral of life with Him.

That provision has been evident in the life of Barry Gates. Gates, who grew up in the Appalachian Mountains in a family with 10 children, was routinely beaten by his alcoholic father, as were his brothers and sisters. His uncles were alcoholics and so was his grandfather. Barry found Christ as a teenager in a mountain church, but he saw some of the same patterns developing in himself that he had seen in his father, uncles, and grandfather. He feared that he had no choice about how he would turn out as a father and that the cycle of abuse and alcoholism would continue. He feared that the cycle was stronger than he was. And he was right.

But it was not stronger than the power of the resurrected Jesus. The family's downward spiral was not broken in one moment—it has taken therapy with Christian counselors, involvement with support groups at the church such as Adult Children of Alcoholics, and most importantly his own commitment to a life with Christ.

"The power of Christ has shown that the cycle can stop with me," he said. "My family now can start a new cycle toward serving God."

Jesus did not wait for Barry to first clean up his life before providing him the power to break the cycle, nor does He wait for us to do the same. By coming to earth, dying, and overcoming death, Jesus did more than just give us hope. He showed us the life-changing power of God available to all of us.

In a way, when the infant Jesus took His first step, He took it toward us. He understands the pain we suffer in this life. He suffers with us. He becomes poor with us. He experiences the rejection, humiliation, and misunderstanding with us. He dies with us. But He does one more thing too. He overcomes death and breaks the cycle of sin, making that power available to us.

Only God could do that.

The Short Course

In the Beginning

God has created us in such a way that we have a built-in longing for Him; we will be satisfied only through a relationship with Him. That built-in desire comes from the Holy Spirit, identified in the story of Adam and Eve as the breath of God.

His Role in Salvation

The Holy Spirit draws us to Christ, convicts us of sin and our need of God's righteousness, causes us to be born anew, and convinces us that we are God's children.

God the Communicator

The Holy Spirit is God in touch with His world. The Spirit was present from the beginning of creation and has been God communicating with His creation ever since. Through the Spirit, God convicts, comforts, and cheers us on.

BACKGROUND
SCRIPTURE:
Gen. 1:26-27; 2:7
Rom. 8:9-11
1 Cor. 2:11-16

**Frank Dewey,
Karen DeSollar,
and
Dean Nelson**

The Spirit for Every Day

The Holy Spirit is not given just for salvation and sanctification but also for daily living. As we wrestle with issues of honesty and integrity, impure thoughts, and temptations to gossip, the Spirit sensitizes our conscience, prods us to faithfulness, and guides us to decisions.

6

Who the Holy Spirit Is and What He Does

He didn't first show up at Pentecost, and His work is not confined to entire sanctification.

ISN'T IT CURIOUS that the world we live in is so adept at providing for our physical, emotional, and intellectual needs but is unable to meet our deep spiritual needs?

Wonder if it's because the world can't provide for our spiritual needs?

We sure can get our physical needs met, for a price. We see advertisements for all sorts of exercise equipment, athletic wear, and liquids to quench the thirsts after a hard workout. We see offers for diets to help us lose weight and to lower our cholesterol counts. Clothing stores help us dress in style. And some physicians help us perfect what we wrap those latest fashions in. They change the shape of our hips and lips, nose and toes, and just about anything else with which we're displeased. They can even put hair on our bald heads.

We get our emotional needs met too. Phone companies encourage us to keep calling home and rekindling relationships that stretch over miles and years. There are thousands of products, professions, and clubs designed to make us laugh, cry, rage, and exult. Greeting card companies know we like to express our emotions to one another, so they provide messages for us—all we have to do is sign our names to the printed words.

We can also get our intellectual needs met. Colleges and universities exist to expand the mind as well as to prepare people for a vocation. There are book clubs all over the world where millions receive books dedicated to enlightening their members. Television seems to contradict the notion that people have intellects, but there are even some programs that acknowledge its viewers are thinking beings.

But what about our spiritual needs? Why the lack of emphasis on the spiritual dimension of humanity? It is obvious that there is a craving in humans for someone or something beyond us, greater than us. Nearly every culture that historians know anything about have worshiped some kind of deity.

Søren Kierkegaard, a Danish philosopher from the early 1800s, wrote, "As the arrow, loosed from the bow by the hand of the practiced archer, does not rest till it has reached the mark, so men pass from God to God. He is the mark for which they have been created, and they do not rest till they find their rest in him" (*Meditations from Kierkegaard*, Westminster Press).

God has created us in such a way that we have a built-in longing for Him; we will be satisfied only through a relationship with Him. But how can God, majestic and holy, the God who "sits enthroned above the circle of the earth" (Isa. 40:22), be in a relationship with us?

God is spirit; we are flesh and blood.

How can the two come together, especially now that Christ is no longer physically on earth to merge heaven with humanity?

They can come together because God has put some of heaven within humanity. He has created us in His image (Gen. 1:27). And He did it through the Holy Spirit.

Surprised? You can read about it in Gen. 2:7. When

God created Adam He "formed the man from the dust of the ground and breathed into his nostrils the breath of life, and the man became a living being." The Old Testament words for "breath," "wind," and "spirit" are the same. This is true in the New Testament as well and is apparent when Jesus tells Nicodemus that people must be "born of water and the Spirit" (John 3:5).

Why Folks Don't Understand What "Spirit" Means

Today, *spirit* is a word often used to describe a person's attitude.

We might compliment a person for having a "sweet spirit," particularly after the person has been insulted or done dirty. So when we hear the word *spirit*, we don't think of a person. In fact, the word *spirit*, in English as well as in other languages, is neuter in gender. It doesn't specify male or female.

But Scripture makes it clear that the Holy Spirit is a person.

The Spirit did not allow Paul to enter certain territories, He taught the disciples, He intercedes on our behalf, and we are warned not to treat Him with disrespect.[1]

In the Old Testament he is referred to as "the Spirit of the Lord" or "of God." And in the New Testament He is called "the Spirit of Jesus," "the Spirit of God," and "the Holy Spirit." He is God, a part of the inseparable Trinity of the Father, Son, and Holy Spirit.

The Holy Spirit is God in touch with His world. The Spirit was present from the beginning of creation and has been God communicating with His creation ever since.

This Spirit is given credit for granting wisdom to people such as Joseph and craftsmanship to Bezalel.[2] The judges and other leaders of Israel, such as kings and prophets, were acknowledged as having the Spirit of God upon them, in being able to carry out God's purposes.

The Spirit's Role

The New Testament gives more detail than the Old Testament about the work of the Holy Spirit, particularly in His role as "go-between" with God and human beings.

The Holy Spirit watches over us and frustrates the attempts of Satan to desensitize our awareness of God. The Spirit also seeks to restore in us the image of God that has been marred by sin. Related to that, Jesus said one of the main functions of the Spirit is to convict the world of sin. For it is only when there is genuine conviction that God's work of salvation and restoration can begin.

Everything God does for us in salvation comes through the Holy Spirit. The Spirit draws us to Christ, convicts us of sin and our need of God's righteousness, causes us to be born anew, and convinces our spirit that we are God's children, thereby providing inner certainty of spiritual reality.

He even prompts us to act in ways that benefit others, sometimes without our knowing He is the one doing the prompting.

A college professor and his wife had a cousin who was dying of AIDS in another state, far enough away that they couldn't visit. This dying man had given his life to Christ two years before being diagnosed with the fatal disease. And as a new Christian, reading the Bible was the activity that brought him the most pleasure during what he knew were his final months. The helpers at the hospice would prop him up and lay his Bible across his lap, because he was too weak to sit up by himself or even to hold the book.

"Let's send him the Bible on cassette tape," the professor's wife suggested. That same day the professor bought a collection of tapes, jotted a note to his cousin, and mailed the package.

Within a few days after the package arrived, the man's

immune system gave way to an infection that caused him to go blind. Reading was impossible. Now he could only listen. And he had his favorite book to listen to.

Coincidence?

The professor doesn't think so.

Perhaps what we have here is evidence that the Holy Spirit is at work at times and in ways in which we are not aware.

Without the Holy Spirit there is no Christian life. Paul puts it this way, "If anyone does not have the Spirit of Christ, he does not belong to Christ" (Rom. 8:9).

Most Christians can accept the fact that the Spirit needs to be at work in our lives. But is it possible for Him to be in complete control? And if so, when does that happen?

Christians in churches that grew out of the theological understanding expressed by Methodist founder John Wesley, such as the Church of the Nazarene, Free Methodist Church, and The Wesleyan Church, teach that Christians can release complete control of their lives to the Holy Spirit. The evidence of Scripture and the experience of Christians throughout the ages suggests this usually takes place sometime after conversion. When Christians have had time to mature in the faith, they often reach an awareness that there are aspects of their lives they have not released to God's control. In such a moment they completely yield control to the Holy Spirit, and they begin to more fully reflect the holy character of God himself.

Gifts of the Spirit

There is a lot of emphasis given by some churches today on the spectacular works of the Holy Spirit, such as healings, of speaking in unintelligible languages, and miracles. These are sometimes called "signs and wonders" or "signs and miracles," particularly by believers called

Charismatics. Most commonly associated with churches in the Pentecostal Movement, such as the Assemblies of God, Charismatics are also in many Protestant churches, as well as in the Roman Catholic Church.

Today, the word *charisma* may mean charm, glamour, or personal magnetism, but in the New Testament it literally means "grace gift" and refers to any of the spiritual endowments Christians have in varying degrees.

The New Testament talks about two categories of gifts.

One category consists of gifts available for all Christians: becoming right with God, eternal life, and other forms of God's mercy.[3]

The other category consists of gifts given to individuals by the Spirit, to serve the Body of Christ in a variety of ways. These gifts, such as teaching, prophesying, and leadership, can be called "service gifts" since they are used by Christians to serve and uplift the Body of believers.[4]

Paul says in 1 Corinthians 12 that it is in the context of the church that the Spirit distributes these gifts for the common good, the mutual uplifting of all believers, and the outreach of the church into the world.

The greatest gift of all, however, is the Holy Spirit himself. For He gives us the wisdom and strength to live a godly life so that we can be what Jesus called the "salt" and "light" of the world (Matt. 5:13-14). The Spirit and the gifts He gives bring about both an internal change toward Christlikeness and an outer service to a needy world.

That internal change is something that takes place every day. The Holy Spirit is not given just for salvation and sanctification but also for daily living. Though there are spiritual mountain-peak experiences, most of our lives take place in the ordinary, daily setting where we wrestle with issues of honesty and integrity, impure thoughts, jealousy, and temptations to gossip. Here we are called to grow in grace and maturity as the Spirit sensitizes our conscience, prods us to faithfulness in prayer and study of God's Word, guides us in decisions major and minor, and strengthens our resolve as a witness in front of a watching world.

Jesus called the Spirit a counselor, advocate, and comforter. These terms show that the Spirit is given to stand alongside us in the experiences of life, for strengthening, encouragement, advice, and comfort. Beyond that, the Spirit even empowers Christians to provide that same kind of service to others.

So the Holy Spirit is at work in more than just the individual's life, important as that is. As He was breathed into the first human being and continues to be breathed into all of creation, God's Spirit unites believers into the Body of Christ we call the church. Through the work of the Spirit we have a united fellowship characterized by study and teaching, prayer and worship, and the sharing of resources (see Acts 2:42-47). It is no wonder that such a Christian community, filled with the Spirit, made such an impression on Jewish religious leaders in the first century that the Christians were accused of turning the world upside down, or, more accurately, right side up.

That same Spirit crosses the boundaries of culture—and even language—as believers take the message of Jesus around the world. Dean Nelson, a contributor to this chapter, tells of such an experience in his book about mission radio programs, *Small Medium, Large Impact*. He visited the Solises, a South American, Spanish-speaking couple who had found Christ through a radio message.

"We sat around the table and prayed, thanking God for the miracle of new life in Him, which we all had now experienced. I prayed in English. They prayed in Spanish. The songbirds in their cages created a deafening background of music. And though we did not understand what the other was saying on one level, the Solises, the birds, and I knew *exactly* what the other was saying! We wept in joy together because God was in that room, and language barriers couldn't keep us from celebrating that presence."[5]

The presence of God is the Spirit of God. We may not always recognize Him among us, but He is here, binding us together, cheering us on, convicting us, comforting us, and convincing us that we are more than physical, emotional, and intellectual beings—we are spiritual beings as well.

Because of the Holy Spirit, we have within us the very breath of God himself.

---

1. Acts 16:6-7; John 14:26; Rom. 8:26-27; Eph. 4:30; Matt. 12:31-32; 1 Cor. 2:11.

2. Gen. 41:38; Exod. 31:3.

3. Rom. 5:15-16; 6:23; 11:29; 1 Cor. 7:7; 2 Cor. 1:11.

4. 1 Cor. 12:7-11; Rom. 12:6-8; Eph. 4:11-13.

5. Dean Nelson, *Small Medium, Large Impact* (Kansas City: Beacon Hill Press of Kansas City, 1993), 93.

The Short Course

Conviction

It's not something dark and negative. It's a warning light God has given us—a dawning awareness that life in sin is not good.

Repentance

It's not the same as confession. Confession is admitting we've done something wrong. Repentance is the decision that changes the direction of our life and keeps us ever headed toward God.

Belief

It's more than thinking God will save us, as He promised. It's acting on that understanding. When we learn to swim, our instructor tells us to relax, because the water will support us. We know in our heads this is true. We've seen others floating by. But we don't trust the water at first. We fight with it, trying to flail ourselves afloat. After we repent of our sins we can trust that God "is faithful and just and will forgive us our sins and purify us from all unrighteousness" (1 John 1:9).

Forgiveness

When God forgives us He treats us as if we had never sinned. It is then we find peace with God.

New Birth

In physical birth, a child who had not existed before comes to life. In spiritual birth, a sinner who was spiritually dead is made alive in Christ.

BACKGROUND SCRIPTURE:
John 3:3
Rom. 3:10-23
2 Cor. 5:17
Eph. 2:4-9; 4:24

Roger Hahn
and
Dean Nelson

7

What Happens When We Become a Christian

Some people have dramatic conversions in which their lives take an about-face. Others, raised in the church, can't remember a time they were headed anywhere but toward Jesus. What could people like this possibly have in common?

JOHN MOORE was the elderly Texan's name. After each service during the week of revival, he had been the center of attention, laughing, joking, smiling—never a serious word. But after the final sermon of the series, he gripped the hand of the speaker: Roger Hahn, one of the contributors to this chapter.

"Powerful sermon, preacher," he said. "I hope you don't think bad of me for jokin' around so much all week. I was 30 before I met the Lord. It was such a wonderful change in my life that I've been wanting to laugh and holler ever since."

John Moore understood the difference Christianity had made in his life. He may not have been able to explain all the theological terms that scholars use to describe the experience, but he knew his life had been changed.

What exactly is it that happens when a person becomes a Christian? And why do we have so much jargon to describe it? We say a person "got saved," "found the Lord," or "accepted Christ." And these are just a few of the less technical phrases. Biblical scholars often use words like *justification, redemption,* and *initial sanctification.*

There are at least two reasons for this wide variety of expressions.

First, the Bible itself uses many different words and phrases to refer to the great change that takes place when a person becomes a Christian.

And second, because humans are so different, there are many ways we can meet Christ.

So we use many expressions to describe the event of becoming a Christian. Common to every new believer is the fact that a big change has taken place. That big change, the one that made John Moore want "to laugh and holler," is often called conversion—the change from sinfulness to righteousness.

Who Likes Being Called a Sinner?

To better understand what it means to become a Christian, let's take a quick look at what human beings are before they begin to follow Christ. In a word, they're sinners.

Our society doesn't take the term sin very seriously. The word sounds as out of date as the Pilgrims on Plymouth Rock. Besides, it doesn't put human beings in a positive light—and today we like to accent the positive.

A noted psychiatrist wrote in *Whatever Became of Sin?:* "The popular leaning is away from notions of guilt and morality . . . Disease and treatment have been the watchwords of the day and little is said about selfishness or guilt or the 'morality gap.' And certainly no one talks about sin!"[1]

But the Bible clearly says that people who have not accepted Christ as Savior are sinners. And, as our culture shows, one of the main characteristics of sin is to deny that a serious problem exists.

"I may not be perfect, but I'm no bank robber either." That would express a typical attitude of today's sinner. The problem is that a person who talks this way assumes that people are sinners because they break God's rules. But the Bible says the opposite. People break God's laws because they are sinners.

A sinner isn't just someone who breaks rules. A sinner is a person who has not put God at the center of his or her life.

As Paul puts it in Rom. 1:25, sinners worship and serve creatures (themselves mostly) rather than the Creator. All sins are expressions of our decision to seize control of our lives. (For quite a list of sins, read Rom. 1:18—3:20.)

We were created in the image of God to worship and obey Him. But sin has managed to distort the very reason for our existence. It twists and bends the person God made us to be and to become, as we described in chapter 1. And when our lives are bent so far from what we were created to be, we don't experience the fellowship with God that we were created to have.

Sometimes that absence of relationship between the Creator and His creation produces behavior as deviant as we would expect from a child raised without the support of a loving adult. We see obsessions, addictions, perversions, uncontrollable anger, and denial. Sometimes the results are not so obvious. Sometimes the lack of relationship with God shows up as a person without a purpose in life.

Becoming a Christian takes a major change—a conversion. Though a change is needed, Rom. 3:10-23 makes it clear that we are not able to make that change by ourselves. "No one will be declared righteous in his sight by observing the law; rather, through the law we become conscious of sin" (v. 20).

That means we are faced with the dilemma of knowing we must change but also knowing that we can't by ourselves. The most devastating result of our sin is our inability to change our own lives and restore the relationship with our Creator. But the good news is that God—and only God—*is* able to change us.

God makes conversion possible for us by granting what theologians call "converting grace" or "saving grace." This is God's power that enables us to do our part in conversion, which is to repent and to have faith that God has saved us.

Conviction Is Not a Bad Thing

For many people, the first awareness of God's "converting grace" surfaces in the form of conviction. That is the dawning awareness that life in sin is not good.

We often paint conviction with dark and negative colors, partly because of what we see in legal proceedings: criminals get "convicted" for their crimes. We may also resist the word because of feelings of artificial guilt. We've heard speakers who talk as if they had the Holy Spirit's job assignment of convicting sinners.

For these reasons, and others, many people try to avoid settings in which they might experience conviction, real or artificial. But conviction from God is a positive thing. It is a warning light flashing on an instrument panel, telling us something is wrong and disaster is ahead if the problem isn't corrected.

Conviction does not take place the same way in every person. For some it is intense and even frightening. Others are barely aware of it. The length of time one is "under conviction" also varies. Conversion, by the way, will end the conviction, but other warning lights could appear at any stage of the Christian life.

1. Repentance is the first human step in conversion. The Bible's idea of repentance means a change of mind that produces a change of direction in life.

D. Paul Thomas, actor, scriptwriter, and producer, says he came under conviction while performing in a secular theater production in Illinois. While in a park across the street from the theater late one night, he says he saw a truck come barreling down the road. Suddenly it came to a screeching halt. The driver threw the gear shift in reverse and pressed down on the gas pedal, making the truck go backward quickly for several feet. The driver turned the truck onto a road he had passed, then sped away.

Thomas says he felt as if God were showing him that he needed to do something similar—step on the brake, change directions, and proceed down a different road. He began his walk with Jesus that night. Since then, he has been the creative force behind productions about the lives of Christian leaders such as Dietrich Bonhoeffer, the theologian and author who was executed in prison in Nazi Germany, and Phineas Bresee, founder of the Church of the Nazarene.

Thomas's change in direction illustrates the Hebrew word for *repentance* in the Old Testament. It means simply "to turn around." Repentance is turning from a life with self at the center, toward a life with God at the center. Eighteenth-century theologian John Wesley called repentance "a change of heart from all sin to all holiness." This change begins with a decision to turn from our old life without God to a life with God. Repentance comes when we take the actions necessary to actually change the patterns and direction of our lives.

Many people confuse repentance with confession of sin. But confession doesn't go far enough. The biblical word for *confess* simply means to agree with God. Confession of sin is agreeing with God that sin is wrong and harmful and that one should stop sinning. The very act of confessing sin often makes people feel better. They "get it off their chests." And the relief of finally being honest with God about the true condition of our sinful lives may feel so good that people stop short of repentance.

But confession is not repentance. Confession agrees that our sin is wrong. Repentance is the decision and the action that changes the direction of our lives and keeps us ever headed toward God. Does it mean we quit our secular job and go into full-time evangelism? Not necessarily. It means we look to God for direction, and we follow Him.

2. After repentance comes belief—the faith that God has saved us. Belief is the act of trusting in God's mercy and power. Believing (or faith, as it is often called) is more than just thinking or knowing that God's word is true. It is acting on that acknowledgment.

For example, when we learn to swim, our instructor tells us to relax, because the water will support us. We know in our heads this is true. We've seen countless others floating comfortably in the water. But we don't trust the water at first; it's new to us. So we fight with it, trying to flail ourselves afloat instead of trusting in the natural buoyancy. And we stay where we can reach the edge of the pool.

We will never learn to swim until we move from the security of the wall and begin to put our confidence in the water's ability to make us float.

Here's another way to describe what it means to believe in God for our salvation. It means switching the control center of our lives from ourselves to God. In other words, a true sign of faith is obedience.

A while back Roger Hahn sent his four-year-old son to his room after the boy misbehaved. When the dad went to discuss the situation with his son, the boy was still angry and unrepentant. But a little while later, when the dad returned a second time, the boy beamed, "It's OK now, Dad. I have a new brain."

That was the child's way of saying he had a new attitude. He had surrendered the right to control the situation himself and had given the right to his dad.

When we refuse to obey God we show that we trust ourselves more than we trust Him. Christians in Wesleyan denominations put great emphasis on obedience, but we do not obey just to prove that we believe. That would be salvation by our own effort or works. Instead, we obey because by faith we have put our full confidence for our salvation in Christ's atoning death on the Cross.

Paul put it this way, "It is by grace you have been saved, through faith—and this not from yourselves, it is the gift of God—not by works, so that no one can boast" (Eph. 2:8-9).

How Conversion Changes Us

God not only enables us to repent and believe but also brings about certain changes in us and for us at conversion.

1. Forgiveness is the change most Protestants mention first. Sometimes the Bible and theologians use a more technical term—*justification*. However, as Wesley declared, "Justification is pardon, the forgiveness of sins."

In forgiveness, God releases us from the punishment due for our sins. *Justification* is a term that portrays God as a judge in a courtroom declaring that the charges against us have been dropped.

Though as human beings we find it hard to forgive and forget, when God forgives us, He treats us as if we had never sinned. His forgiveness sets us free from the paralyzing guilt and fear that can come when we realize we have sinned against God.

Brennan Manning, author of *The Ragamuffin Gospel*,

tells about a woman who was reported to have had visions of Jesus. A religious man decided to check her out.

"Is it true, m'am, that you have visions of Jesus?" asked the cleric.

"Yes," the woman replied simply.

The man told her to ask Jesus, next time He appeared, to tell her the sins that the man had recently confessed.

"You actually want me to ask Jesus to tell me the sins of your past?" she asked.

"Exactly. Please call me if anything happens."

Ten days later the woman called, saying Jesus had appeared. The man rushed to her house.

"I asked Jesus to tell me the sins you confessed," the woman said.

The man leaned forward with anticipation. His eyes narrowed.

"What did Jesus say?"

She took his hand and gazed deep into his eyes. "These are his exact words: 'I CAN'T REMEMBER.'"[2]

Justification, a New Testament concept, has a rich, Old Testament heritage. Paul and the writer of Hebrews both quote Hab. 2:4, which says the just will live by faith. This is a reminder that conversion is not accomplished by our own effort—it's not what we get by keeping all the rules. As the swimmer must relax and, by faith, trust the water to provide the flotation, sinners must relax and trust God's plan for salvation rather than trying to save themselves.

2. We become reconciled to God and are no longer at odds with Him or His plans for our life.

When God forgives us, our relationship with Him changes. As sinners we were at odds with God's purpose. That is part of what it means to be a sinner. Reconciliation is the end of being at odds and the beginning of peace. Rom. 5:1 says, "Since we have been justified through faith, we have peace with God."

3. Another way to describe the change in relationship with God is to call it a *new birth*.

Other similar terms are *regeneration* or *born again*. Jesus spoke of this to Nicodemus, saying, "I tell you the truth, no one can see the kingdom of God unless he is born again" (John 3:3).

Forgiveness describes a change in the way God treats us. But the new birth describes an actual change within us. We are born spiritually into a new life of relationship with God.

In physical birth, a child who had not existed before comes to life. In spiritual birth, a sinner who was spiritually dead is made alive in Christ. Paul talks about this in Eph. 2:1-7, saying that "because of his great love for us, God, who is rich in mercy, made us alive with Christ even when we were dead in transgressions" (vv. 4-5).

The new birth idea is especially important for a Wesleyan understanding of conversion. Many Protestants preach and live in such a way that suggests forgiveness is the only purpose of conversion. But Wesleyans believe the new birth opens the door that allows us to be restored to the holiness known by Adam at creation.

Forgiveness changes our standing in the eyes of God and releases us from being condemned to the penalty for our sins. And the new birth builds on the truth of this. We are to "put on the new self, created to be like God in true righteousness and holiness" (Eph. 4:24).

For this reason, Wesleyans consider the new birth as the first step of being made holy. To use another technical term, the new birth is also called initial sanctification. It's not entire sanctification, but it leads toward it (entire sanctification will be discussed in detail in a later chapter).

When a baby is born, a relative will sometimes say, "She looks just like Grandma," or "He looks just like his dad." Actually, the infant doesn't usually resemble that person much at all. But certain features suggest that the child will someday grow up to look like Grandma or Dad. Likewise, a newly born Christian is given characteristics that can grow and develop in Christlikeness. Experienced observers will see that potential and may even say that the new convert has been made like Christ. That is why Wesleyans speak of the new birth as including initial sanctification. A sinner who is born again is, at conversion, given the spiritual "genes" to be holy. But a lifetime of growing into that holiness awaits.

Wrong Ideas About Conversion

As many ways as the New Testament speaks of conversion and as many ways as people experience God's grace, it is no wonder that misunderstanding occurs. We'll mention three.

1. Sometimes one aspect of conversion is emphasized and other important aspects are left out.

Overemphasis on forgiveness, for example, and underemphasis on the new birth produces Christians who are confident of being right with God but whose lives do not give evidence of it.

Overemphasis on new birth and underemphasis on forgiveness can lead to Christians who talk about experiences with God but who don't repent of their sins when new warning lights come on.

2. Some Christians have mistakenly understood that baptism is necessary for salvation. In some places the New Testament speaks of baptism as if it were the same as conversion. For example, in speaking of the Flood, Peter says, "This water symbolizes baptism that now saves you" (1 Pet. 3:21). And Jesus says, "Go and make disciples of all nations, baptizing them in the name of the Father and of the Son and of the Holy Spirit" (Matt. 28:19).

There were no unbaptized Christians in New Testament times. Since Jesus had commanded baptism, the first Christians baptized people as soon as they were converted. The story of the Ethiopian treasurer, in Acts 8:35-38, shows how quickly baptism was done. So, in the New Testament, baptism was not regarded as merely a ritual or as only an outward act. Rather, it was a dramatic and effective way of communicating the reality that God had changed the sinner's life. It was not, however, essential to conversion. The Christians were converted before the water touched them.

As long as the Church evangelized Jews and God-loving Gentiles, who had been taught the Old Testament commandments, baptism at the time of conversion worked well. These people had at least an acquaintance with the idea of godliness. But when Christianity began to attract converts who were pagans with no moral training, the church began to delay baptism until the convert had finished a time of training in basic Christian living and beliefs.

This brought a subtle shift in the understanding of baptism. Rather than communicating the forgiving, cleansing grace of God, it became for many in the Early Church a symbol of human faith. In either case, however, it is a proper ritual to observe. But it does not save us. "It is by grace you have been saved, through faith—and this not from yourselves, it is the gift of God" (Eph. 2:8)

3. Another misunderstanding is that conversion has to happen to all people the same way.

While the majority of Christians came to faith through a crisis experience, there are some godly people who have no memory of such a crisis event. In the first generation of Christianity, all converts came from either Judaism or the pagan world. However, after the first generation of Christians came a second generation, raised within the faith. They were called to turn from their sins to Christ, but they did not need to convert (literally, to "change religions").

They decided to continue following Christ, as they had been taught from childhood.

Some individuals from second, third, and later generations of Christian families may not remember a time of sinful rebellion in their lives. They testify that they have always wanted to follow Christ and that they can't remember a time when they weren't committed to the Lord.

This is a beautiful testimony. We should not demand that such people be "converted" in the same way as people who have lived sinful lives, knowing that they were separated from God.

This does not mean that people raised in the church have never sinned. It does mean that for some the decision to follow Christ did not require an emotional crisis.

There are many different ways to describe what it means to become a Christian. The common theme is that life with Christ is far different from life without Him. The apostle Paul expressed that difference well when he wrote, "If anyone is in Christ, he is a new creation; the old has gone, the new has come!" (2 Cor. 5:17).

Paul knew what he was talking about. Once a persecutor of Christians, he had became a leader of them.

God still makes new creations.

---

1. Karl Menninger, *Whatever Became of Sin?* (New York: Hawthorne Books, 1973), 35.

2. Adapted from Brennan Manning, *The Ragamuffin Gospel* (Portland, Oreg.: Multnomah Press, 1990), 116-17.

The Short Course

What Is It?

Wesleyans believe that, after conversion, but before death, a believer's heart may be cleansed from all sin.

So Sanctified People Can't Sin?

They can sin, just like Adam and Eve could sin. But they are more likely not to sin. Before entire sanctification, people have a tendency toward sinning and selfishness. Afterward, they have a tendency toward righteousness.

BACKGROUND
SCRIPTURE:
Lev. 19:2
Acts
Rom. 6:1-12
1 Thess. 5:23
1 John 2:1-2

**Howard Culbertson,
Roger Hahn,
and
Dean Nelson**

How Perfect Is "Christian Perfection"?

Not as perfect as many seem to think. The Bible's word for *perfect* means that a person is as complete as he or she was designed to be at that moment. A seven-year-old piano player might perform a one-handed version of a song perfectly. And the piano teacher might say, "Perfect!" But when that musician reaches 27, the teacher is going to expect something more.

8

How Entire Is Entire Sanctification?

It's the distinctive teaching of churches in the Holiness Movement. Yet, inside the movement and out, it is one of the most misunderstood teachings of all.

JONATHAN HAHN has always been more motivated by recess than by any other of his classes. Take it from his dad, one of the contributors to this chapter.

For an hour one day in second grade, Jonathan had avoided working his math sheet. Then the teacher told him that every problem would have to be done before he could go out for recess. Within two minutes, his teacher reported, he had written an answer for every problem. Unfortunately every answer was wrong, and the teacher sent the work sheet home for him to do over.

"You'll have to do all these problems again," his dad told him.

"Why?" he asked.

"They're all wrong," his dad replied.

"So?" he shrugged. "Nobody's perfect."

Jonathan's final phrase pretty well sums up why some people reject entire sanctification. Even bumper stickers proclaim, "Christians aren't perfect—just forgiven." And those who need more authority than a bumper sticker turn to 1 John 1:8, which clearly states, "If we claim to be without sin, we deceive ourselves and the truth is not in us."

Why Teach Entire Sanctification?

So in the face of conventional wisdom, bumper stickers, and 1 John 1:8, why do Christians in Wesleyan denominations insist on teaching entire sanctification?

Because the Bible teaches perfect love, a pure heart, and freedom from slavery to sin. These, and several other terms, are concepts that entire sanctification refers to.

The possibility of deliverance from all sin and of being renewed in the image of God are themes that permeate the Scriptures. Take prayers in the Bible, for instance. They contain the cries of people seeking a holy relationship with God (Psalm 51; John 17:17-23); Paul prayed that sanctification was his heart's desire for the people of Thessalonica. "May God himself, the God of peace, sanctify you through and through" (1 Thess. 5:23).

Beyond the prayers of people longing for holiness are the Bible's commands that we be holy. "Be holy because I, the LORD your God, am holy" is the first of several passages that call us to spiritual maturity (Lev. 19:2; see also Matt. 5:48 and Heb. 6:1).

The Bible also contains examples of people who lived in holy relationship with God. Noah was "a righteous man, blameless" (Gen. 6:9). Job was "blameless and upright" (Job 1:1). First John 4:17 says, "Love has been perfected among us" (NRSV).

There are plenty of other verses we could list as evidence of the biblical teaching on holiness. (See especially the Book of Acts.) But more important is that the whole fabric of the Bible portrays a vision of a people set apart into a holy relationship with our holy God.

The message of the Bible is not the bad news of defeat and enslavement to sin or of the awfulness of humanity.

Rather, Scripture sings out the optimistic Good News that the grace of God is working to bring us victory over sin and into a holy, joyful relationship with Him—the relationship we were created to have in the beginning.

Why Is It So Hard to Understand?

One reason people have such a hard time understanding the teaching is because of the wide variety of terms we use to explain it: perfect love, Christian perfection, holiness—to name a few.

Sometimes it appears that Holiness theologians are saying that all the terms refer to the same experience. At other times, they want to be sure we understand the different meanings and nuances of the terms. No wonder people are perplexed.

The confusion is a bit like the "system overload" a young sportswriter experienced at a recent sports journalism conference in Florida. A group of high school sports writers from around the country joined seasoned professionals in covering a National Hockey League game between the Tampa Bay Lightning and the Buffalo Sabres. The student from Mississippi had never seen a hockey game and asked a barrage of questions about the rules. A hockey writer nearby tried to explain the meaning of offsides, icing, a two-line pass, and penalties that were unique to the game. The student grew visibly irritated at the complexity of the event, and the irritation evolved into boredom. The young man finally pulled out his headphones and cassette player, abandoning his effort to understand.

Suddenly, as is the custom of hockey games, a fight broke out among the players. The student nudged the writer enthusiastically.

"Now this part of the game I understand!" he said.

We don't need a fight to break out in the church to

help everyone understand entire sanctification. In fact, a fight over holiness would really complicate things. But we do need a good dose of explanation that everyone can understand.

Here is what Wesleyan Christians believe, which many other Christians do not believe: After conversion, but before death, a believer's heart may be cleansed from all sin. The expressions "entire sanctification," "perfect love," and "Christian perfection" are some of the terms Wesleyans use to describe this experience.

The words "entire" and "perfect" have often led to misunderstanding of this doctrine. So to help clarify these and other areas of misunderstanding, we'll try asking—and answering—the questions we think you'd like to ask.

Why is the experience called *entire sanctification?*

It's called *sanctification* because that's the biblical word for the act of being made holy, which begins at the new birth and continues until death. And it's called *entire* because in 1 Thess. 5:23 Paul prays that the God of peace will sanctify the people "entirely" (NRSV) or "wholly" (RSV).

John Wesley understood this and often spoke of the experience of being sanctified "entirely" or "wholly."

This creates a problem. How can one point in that process be called *entire* if there is further sanctification afterward? As we can see through Scripture, though sanctification begins in a moment, growth in becoming more like Christ happens throughout one's lifetime.

Why is the word *perfect* used for this experience?

John Wesley himself said that the only reason he did not drop this word is because the Bible spoke of perfection. Wesley, however, did insist that the words *perfect* and *perfection* never be used by themselves to describe the experience. He demanded that his followers speak of *Christian perfection* rather than *perfection* and *perfected in love* rather than just *perfected.*

The biblical words for *perfect* and *perfection* do not mean absolute perfection in which no improvement is possible. The biblical words mean that a person or thing is as complete as it was designed or expected to be at that moment.

One illustration of this is the marriage relationship. When two people decide to get married, they make a commitment to one another and decide that they will no longer live their lives separate from one another. The day of their wedding the marriage relationship is as complete as it can be that day. As the weeks and months of marriage continue, the couple can grow in the relationship.

Was this couple's relationship less complete on the wedding day than it was at an anniversary many years later? No. It was as complete as it could be at each moment.

That is what Christian perfection is like, as we grow each day in our relationship with God. We are perfect at each moment of growth, as a result of having a perfect God residing in us.

Here's another example. A little girl might play a simple one-hand piece on the piano for her first recital. The teacher could well exclaim, "That was perfect!" Years later the grown woman, as an accomplished musician, could not play the same simple piece and have it called perfect. Much more would be expected of her.

Likewise, when a person comes to love God with an undivided heart, the Bible says this is perfect love. That does not mean that no further growth is possible. In fact, the contrary is true. Once we love perfectly, or completely, that's when growth becomes possible.

What happens to sin when I am entirely sanctified?

Sin, in the sense of worshiping self instead of God, rules the life of an unbeliever. In conversion, the ruling power of sin is broken, but the results of that life of sin remain.

Wesley described this sin that remains in believers as including things like pride, self-will, and inappropriate desires. These are not outward acts that break the commands of Scripture. Wesley taught that such blatant sins stopped when a person was converted.

The sin remaining in believers, he said, reflects a disposition or tendency of the heart toward self-centeredness rather than God-centeredness. Entire sanctification cleanses the heart of this self-centeredness, bringing victory over this sin that remains in the believer. To describe what happens here, Wesley used Paul's words in Rom. 6:11-12: "Count yourselves dead to sin but alive to God in Christ Jesus. Therefore do not let sin reign in your mortal body so that you obey its evil desires."

Does this mean that an entirely sanctified person cannot sin?

No, it doesn't. Entire sanctification is not a Wesleyan form of eternal security, teaching that once we're in we're in for good.

The point of entire sanctification is to restore people to the kind of holiness that Adam and Eve enjoyed before the Fall. They had a perfect relationship with God. Yet they chose to sin.

Entire sanctification means that a person's tendency (some call it "bent") is toward righteousness rather than toward sinning. The goal and the reasonable expectation of the entirely sanctified life is to not sin, as 1 John 2:1 makes clear: "My dear children, I write this to you so that you will not sin." The expectation was that the believers would live as Christ lived and do His will. But sanctified people not only do the will of God but also *want* to do the will of God.

What if I do sin?

First John 2:1-2 answers that question. Confess it, seek forgiveness, stop doing it, and accept Christ's atonement.

We should resist the temptation to deny that we have

sinned, if indeed we have. And we should keep from giving sin a less offensive name, such as *mistake*, to downplay it. (By the same token, we do not call honest mistakes or poor judgment "sin.")

Sins of unbelievers and Christians alike violate the law of God and need the atoning blood of Christ. But the sins need not, according to Wesley, break the relationship between the believer and God.

How does entire sanctification take place?

A believer who does not "hunger and thirst for righteousness," as Jesus said in Matt. 5:6, is not a candidate for entire sanctification. The experience comes only after the new birth and growth in grace.

Wesley cautioned against preaching this experience to believers who were not pressing on toward the goal of spiritual maturity mentioned in Phil. 3:14.

Total commitment, sometimes called entire consecration, is the necessary human preparation for entire sanctification.

Entire sanctification involves spiritual maturity, so there is a gradual leading up to it. But since it is also death to sin, there is a noticeable crisis or instant in which the experience takes place.

Some people say they can point to more than one occasion when this death occurred. However, Wesley compared death to sin with a physical death. A person may be dying for some time, but there is an instant when life ceases. Likewise, a person may be gradually dying to sin for some time and becoming more Christlike. But Wesley said there is a point when that death finally happens and the believer becomes dead to sin.

Paul Pate, a 45-year-old landscaper, husband, and father of three in San Diego, describes his experience of entire sanctification. He had been a Christian for 20 years, but only in the last year or so did it begin to gnaw at him that he was missing something in his spiritual life.

"I was a believer—I had a powerful conversion experience—but there was no power in my life," he said. "I rationalized when it came to sin, instead of being victorious over it. I was like everyone else around me: good folks who love God, love our neighbors, share our testimony when asked, and focus our lives on our rents, mortgage payments, jobs, and getting ahead."

After spending a lot of time in God's Word, he came upon Deut. 4:28-29: "There you will worship gods made by human hands out of wood and stone, gods that can neither see nor hear, neither eat nor smell. But if from there you seek the LORD your God, you will find him, if indeed you search with all your heart and soul" (NEB).

"I was so dissatisfied with my life at that point, and when I read this I decided that is what I wanted," he said. "I felt like I only knew God as a concept, and now Jesus was saying to me what He said to His disciples in John 14: 'Have I been with you so long and you still don't know Me?'

"I wanted to know Christ as I had never known Him before."

Driving on a two-lane highway home from his sister's house in Ramona, Calif., more than a year after his search began, Paul said, "I connected."

The presence of God filled his truck in such a way that Paul began to weep. "On that drive I reached a new level of intimacy. And then I wondered how I could have known Christ so long and missed this!"

Brennan Manning described a similar experience in his book *The Ragamuffin Gospel*. He was on a winter retreat, and one thought resounded in him throughout the time of solitude.

"Jesus did not say this on Calvary, though he could have, but he is saying it now; 'I'm dying to be with you.

I'm really dying to be with you,'" Manning wrote. "It was as if he were calling to me for a second time. I realized that what I thought I knew was straw. I had scarcely glimpsed, I had never dreamed what his love could be. The Lord drove me deeper into solitude seeking not tongues, healing, prophecy, or good religious experience each time I prayed, but *understanding* and the quest for pure, passionate Presence."*

More important than human consecration and the length of time involved is the fact that God entirely sanctifies. Cleansing from sin is not something we do for ourselves; it is a gift from God. But because it is God's gift there is a certain mystery to it. We cannot schedule entire sanctification to happen at our command.

What's left after entire sanctification?

Entire sanctification is not the final goal of the Christian life. It's a beginning point—a vital step in the lifelong process of being made more like Christ.

John Wesley put it this way: justification (forgiveness of sins) is the porch; entire sanctification is the door; but the house is full fellowship with God.

So, entire sanctification is the way we enter the fullness of the Christian life. The door is not where we're headed; we want to get inside the house so that we can enjoy full fellowship with God.

Maintaining full fellowship with God is something the apostle Paul said was his lifelong passion. "Not that I have already obtained all this, or have already been made perfect, but I press on to take hold of that for which Christ Jesus took hold of me" (Phil. 3:12).

What happens to me when I am entirely sanctified?

Wesley said that entire sanctification enabled people to love God with their whole heart, soul, mind, and strength, and to love their neighbors as themselves (Mark 12:30-31).

Wesley observed that a person who had entered the experience usually felt a great sense of joy and peace. However, he also noticed that most who had experienced entire sanctification eventually encountered fluctuations—peaks and valleys—in their sense of joy and peace.

Though entire sanctification radically changes our desire and ability to show love, it rarely changes our basic personality. "Driven" sinners usually become "driven" Christians, and they may remain so through a lifetime of sanctification. Laid-back sinners usually become laid-back Christians who rarely show outward signs of excitement when they are entirely sanctified. Malcolm Shelton, a retired religion professor, often said that some people are better by nature than others are by grace.

Unfortunately, many tend to make their own experiences the rule for all others, so the search for evidences of entire sanctification has led to some unpleasant results. Many people have become discouraged and have given up hope of being entirely sanctified because their personalities would not allow them to match another person's experience. Recognizing the variety of ways the work of sanctification comes to individuals can help us restore this hope.

From the time of Wesley, in the 1700s, on through today, some people who believed they were entirely sanctified have shown unusual responses. Shouting, running, jumping, and weeping have all been described—and in some cases promoted—as evidences of entire sanctification. But people with such physical demonstrations have had no better track record at growth in grace following entire sanctification than people who had no noticeable responses. Outward responses are not a dependable confirmation of the inward work of sanctification.

The teaching of some Christians today that speaking in tongues is evidence of entire sanctification cannot be supported either by Scripture or by experience.

The real evidence of entire sanctification cannot be precisely measured by human beings. For the evidence is increasing Christlikeness, in which the image of God is increasingly visible in a believer's life.

Will there be people in heaven who have not experienced entire sanctification?

1. Heaven is not reserved just for Wesleyans or for those who use the phrase "entire sanctification."

Plenty of devoted Christians outside the Wesleyan movement have found this kind of relationship with Christ. Leaders like Billy Graham and Lloyd John Ogilvie, neither of whom would consider themselves Wesleyan, tell about having a second and distinct experience of sanctifying grace. None of these leaders use Wesleyan terminology, but the testimonies are easily recognized by people in Wesleyan circles. But too often such testimonies are the exception rather than the expectation—at least in churches where the doctrine of entire sanctification is not taught.

2. Since Wesley taught there was usually a period of maturing that must occur between the moment of salvation and the work of sanctification, there may be some in heaven who were in this "in between" period when they died. Eternal life is promised to all those who have believed.

3. However, for those who have been saved and have knowingly rejected the Holy Spirit's leading into entire sanctification, a heavenly destination may not be guaranteed. We are called to walk in all the light that has been revealed to us.

The idea of sinning every day in thought, word, and deed is so much less than the victory over sin that the Bible promises. Through the years many Christians have settled for too little, emphasizing human frailness and the pervasiveness of sin. Caving into the argument that a person is doomed to stumble along in constant failure, they have lived defeated lives. Some have given up Christianity altogether. Not only did individuals suffer personal defeat, but there is no telling how far back the kingdom of God has been set.

As human beings, we were created in the image of God to live in holy fellowship with Him. Much of that fellowship was lost to sin. But the experience of heart holiness offers us restoration to God's original plan.

Because of this, genuine, wholehearted love for God, our neighbors, and the rest of His creation is possible for us again. The doctrine of entire sanctification is the door that can lead us into that glorious, full, perfect fellowship with God.

---

*Brennan Manning, *The Ragamuffin Gospel* (Portland, Oreg.: Multnomah Press, 1990), 168.

The Short Course

Resurrected Bodies

The body Jesus had after the Resurrection—a body that could be touched, yet materialize from out of nowhere—is the kind of body Christians can expect in heaven.

Heaven and Hell

We don't know exactly what heaven and hell will be like. Because they will be like nothing we've seen before, we have no frame of reference for comparison. So the Bible uses language and symbols we understand to convey the ideas of incomprehensible majesty and indescribable horror.

The Second Coming

We have no idea what day Jesus will return; in fact, He and others in the Bible tell us to stop wasting our energy speculating. But His return is certain.

BACKGROUND
SCRIPTURE:
Matt. 13:5-30
1 Thess. 5:1-11
2 Pet. 3:9-12
Rev. 21:10-21

Jirair Tashjian
and
Vicki Hesterman

9

Life After Death

What should we make of near-death experiences, Christ's delayed return, and streets of gold in heaven?

"I KNOW WE'LL SEE HIM AGAIN in heaven, but I miss him now," sobbed Patricia, a high school cheerleader. Her boyfriend, Donnie, had been killed in a car accident on a country road near his home in Ohio. Both were teenagers and Christians. They had grown up together and talked of getting married. But the service their pastor conducted was not a wedding; it was a funeral.

There, he spoke of the assurance that Donnie would spend eternity with the Lord. Although the young man's family and friends were grief-stricken at the unexpected separation, they took comfort in knowing there would come a day of reunion in heaven.

Christians believe the dead will be raised up as Christ was raised from the dead. This is different from the kind of immortality of the soul taught by some religions today and by Greek philosophers a few centuries before Christ. Greeks divided a person into two parts, body and soul. They said the body dies and decays because it is evil but the soul lives on forever because it is good. Unfortunately, the soul has no body and no individuality; it is absorbed into the universe and becomes a bit like a single cell in a giant, living organism.

The Christian faith, on the other hand, teaches that

resurrected people are whole beings. Eternal life for Christians involves more than just immortality of the soul. It includes resurrection of the body, which the Greeks could not imagine and would scoff at. Our dead and decaying bodies will be resurrected when Christ comes.

How do we know?

Our physical bodies belong to God. He is the Creator and Re-Creator. We see evidence of what He can do when we look at the resurrection of Jesus. Christ's resurrected body could be recognized and touched, but it could also suddenly materialize into a room or ascend into the sky (Luke 24:36, 51).

The resurrected body is not just the old body brought back to life. It is a new, heavenly, perfect body much like Christ's resurrected body; it is not subject to death. God reverses what natural processes have done and brings life out of death. It is like a live plant growing out of a seed that has fallen in the ground and rotted. Just as God raised Christ from the dead, so will He raise up those who trust in Christ (1 Corinthians 15).

Near-Death: Glimpses into the Future?

Is it possible that people who have had near-death or out-of-body experiences have gone back and forth between an earthly and a heavenly mode of existence? And if so, is this further evidence of life after death? Answers are hard to come by; physicians and theologians are only beginning to study this engaging phenomenon.

Ray Cordes, a stable, sensible, 70-year-old Christian, was hit by a car and thrown 50 feet. He nearly died. The tall, healthy former farmer had been working in his second career as a traveling representative for a Christian magazine. He was crossing a street in a small Michigan town when the car, driven by a 16-year-old driver, struck him.

For days, doctors didn't hold much hope. At one

point, Cordes was on 10 different monitors and machines. He later told his wife, Paula, and other family members about floating above the hospital, accurately describing scenes he couldn't have seen from his bed, even if he had been conscious. He explained how the hallway was laid out and what was in specific rooms, as if he had looked down into the building. He recalled feeling an incredible peace and seeing a bright light. Then he remembered somewhat reluctantly coming back to the room and into his body. Christians all over the country had prayed for his recovery, and he lived to describe his amazing experience.

Pete, a rugged-looking, dark-haired father of three, from Toledo, Ohio, was only 30 when his heart stopped beating after a severe heart attack. He told his family (and later, church groups) of floating above his body and of watching the doctors and nurses working on him in a big Toledo hospital. But he said it wasn't frightening.

"Imagine the most beautiful colors you have ever seen and beautiful music surrounding you. That's the closest I can come to describing the feeling," he recalled.

He didn't want to come back to his body, but he said he believes his work here wasn't done. Pete was a believer before, but now a special peace radiates from him. When his time comes, he says, he's not afraid to die.

The Bible says people will die only one time (Heb. 9:27). But could it be that in these near-death circumstances these Christians experienced a preview of the coming of Christ and the joys of the future resurrection?

Getting Past Speculation on Heaven, Hell, and Christ's Return

How can we describe otherworldly places and events that are unlike anything we have ever known or experienced?

The Bible often does it with imagery, especially when

speaking about the Christian's future hope. For example, the Book of Revelation says heaven is a city in the shape of a cube; in ancient literature, a cube with its equal dimensions was a symbol of perfection.

Other images convey the beauty and endlessness of life with Christ. The foundation of this city, often called the New Jerusalem, is decorated with jewels (Revelation 21). On the city's walls of jasper are 12 gates of pearl. Inside is a street paved with pure gold, along with a river of life and a tree of life.

These descriptions are a way of explaining heavenly reality to people still limited to time and space on planet Earth. Whether there will be a literal street of gold is beyond our ability to know. What we can be sure of is that the beauty, joy, and peace of heaven will surpass our most vivid imagination.

Scripture also describes the final judgment as a lake of fire that burns with sulfur. This graphically portrays the unimaginable horror of being eternally separated from God.

Many sincere Christians spend a great deal of time and energy trying to analyze just when the end of this world will come. In fact, we can become so obsessed with predicting Christ's second coming that we fail to live each day to the fullest as Christ's witnesses. We can also undermine the reputation of Christianity when we make bold predictions that don't come true.

During the height of the Desert Storm war in 1991, the pastor of a large Oklahoma City church announced his sermon topic in the *Daily Oklahoman:* "Iraq: A Major Power in Biblical Prophecy of the End of Time."

He went on to list his main points: "Biblical prophecy reveals that Iraq will be a major military and economic power . . . The capital of Antichrist will be there . . . The ingredients for World War III."

The topic of another of his sermons was "Iraq: The Road to Armageddon." This pastor thought the Iraq war was somehow connected to the end time, World War III, and Armageddon—the final war between good and evil.

Many times in the history of the church, people have set dates for the second coming of Christ. Recently, a Korean pastor did it. As a result, some 20,000 Korean Christians in 1992 sold their belongings, quit their jobs, and waited for Christ's coming. The Korean government anticipated what would happen and put their security forces on alert to help prevent mass suicides.

Setting dates for the Second Coming is not profitable. Jesus himself said, "It is not for you to know the times or dates the Father has set by his own authority" (Acts 1:7).

Yet, we cannot completely ignore questions about Christ's second coming. People are naturally curious about their eternal destiny. What is our future? Why is the coming of Christ taking so long? What happens to us when we die? These are legitimate questions.

However, Wesleyan theology does not accept many of the answers that come from so-called prophecy experts. Biblical prophecy, particularly the Book of Revelation, is not so much a wall chart of people, countries, and events of the last days as it is a word of hope and assurance. This word was important for those to whom it was first addressed centuries ago, when Romans were persecuting and killing Christians. And it is still important. But imposing current events into the ancient message can lead to wrong and even damaging conclusions.

What's Jesus Waiting For?

We hear a lot about the coming of Jesus being very near. We sing "The King Is Coming" and "I'll Fly Away." But we also wonder why Jesus is taking so long.

The mystery seems even more puzzling when we realize Jesus said, "I tell you the truth, this generation will certainly not pass away until all these things have happened" (Matt. 24:34; Mark 13:30; Luke 21:32). But "all these things," if they refer to His Second Coming and the end of the world, did not happen in His generation or since.

The meaning of His statement becomes clearer if we consider related statements in the Gospels.

In Mark 9:1, Jesus says, "I tell you the truth, some who are standing here will not taste death before they see the kingdom of God come with power." But people who were standing in the crowd, and millions of others since then, have died without seeing Jesus come again.

Jesus was either wrong or was talking about something other than the Second Coming.

The fact is, He was talking about some seeing the kingdom of God coming in power. In Mark 1:15, He says, "The time has come . . . The kingdom of God is near." This shows that the kingdom of God was not something way off in the future; it was happening already in Christ's ministry.

Now the meaning of Mark 9:1 becomes clearer. The kingdom of God had already come in power through Christ's resurrection and the presence of the living Christ among His followers.

When Jesus said, "This generation will certainly not pass away until all these things have happened" He was referring, at least in part, to wars, persecutions, pagan desecration of the Temple, false messiahs, and false prophets (Mark 13:5-23). All these did, in fact, happen in that first generation—before and during the fall of Jerusalem in A.D. 70. Jews rebelled against the Roman occupiers, and Rome responded by destroying the entire city, Temple and all.

The second part of Mark 13, verses 24-27, is introduced with the word "but," which expresses a strong contrast. These verses speak of heavenly phenomena, such as the darkening of the sun, moon, and stars, and the coming of the Son of Man in clouds and the gathering of His people. Obviously, not all of these things have happened yet.

So there are still some dramatic events ahead, and we must stay alert. But Mark knew that the end times had already begun in Jesus' life, death, and resurrection. Furthermore, through the preaching of the gospel, Christ was already gathering His people into His Church, the community of faith. So we *are* in the end times, but we have been ever since Christ came to earth.

The second coming of Christ is not just an ushering in of the end times. It is the continuation and completion of what God began through Jesus Christ. Whenever we speak of the Second Coming as though it is only a future event, we miss its connection to the greatness of God's past activity in our world through His people in the Old Testament, Jesus Christ in the New Testament, and the work of the Holy Spirit in the world now.

The Second Coming is a little like a college graduation. A student would be foolish to think of that two-hour ceremony as the sum total of education and do nothing but wait for it. Long years of study and preparation precede that joyous event. Likewise, the coming of Christ is only the final event in God's long history of saving human beings.

People who speculate when, where, and how Christ will come again are focusing their energies on secondary issues. Yet, even Christians in the lifetime of the apostle Paul were doing this. They were apparently quitting their jobs and remaining idle to wait for the coming of the Lord. Paul told them to get to work, be diligent and alert, love and encourage one another, and joyfully wait for the coming of the Lord, without making a big fuss about signs of "times and dates" (1 Thess. 5:1-11).

It may be that the second coming of Christ will not be

what even we Christians imagine. After all, His first coming was so different from what was expected that many people did not see how Jesus could possibly be the promised Messiah.

However, the New Testament does speak of the coming of Christ. Paul, for example, says when Christ returns believers will be taken up in the clouds. Some Christians have come to refer to this as the Rapture. We do not have all the details we may wish concerning the when, where, and how of Jesus' second coming, but there is no doubt He will come again. The Bible says, simply and powerfully, Christ will return.

Wesleyans and non-Wesleyans part company in their understanding of God's plans for the future.

Many non-Wesleyans feel God has the future all mapped out. He has already decided when and how the Second Coming will occur.

Wesleyans leave the future open. They say this is more consistent with biblical theology because in the Bible God sometimes changes His mind, for the benefit of His creation. This was clearly the case when God decided not to destroy the Ninevites but to be merciful to them because they repented after hearing Jonah's preaching.

Wesleyans believe that human decisions have a bearing on when or how Christ will come. God delays the day of Christ's coming to allow more people to repent, according to 2 Pet. 3:9. Verses 11 and 12 go on to say that we human beings can speed up the day of the Lord by living holy and godly lives. The day of Christ's coming is not chiseled into God's marble calendar; because of His grace, the date is not predetermined.

Jesus will come again, and it will be an occasion for rejoicing. Christians who die before the Second Coming will be resurrected. And all believers, living and dead, will be made entirely perfect, body and soul.

After Jesus ascended to heaven, the advice of the angels to the disciples was to stop gazing into the sky (Acts 1:11). Instead, they were to get busy and carry out the plan Jesus gave them: be His witnesses.

We can't prepare for Christ's second coming by searching for signs, making time charts, and trying to figure out the decor of heaven.

We do it by discovering that the kingdom of God has already started and that we are called to be part of it by doing the very same thing the first disciples did: becoming Christ's witnesses.

The Short Course

Why We Go to Church

Christians are called to be a chosen people who serve God. It's hard to be a people by yourself. We need others to teach, learn from, pray with, praise with, fellowship with, and draw encouragement from.

The Church's Job

"Do good works, which God prepared in advance for us to do" (Eph. 2:10). "Go into all the world and preach the good news to all creation" (Mark 16:15). "Love your neighbor as yourself" (Lev. 19:18).

Which Church Is It?

Because there are so many dimensions to the church, descriptions can appear contradictory. The church is divine and human, visible and invisible, fighting and victorious, universal and local.

BACKGROUND
SCRIPTURE:
Luke 4:18-19
Acts 2:42-47
Eph. 4:7-16

Lyle Pointer,
Vicki Hesterman,
and
Dean Nelson

10

Why People Need the Church

And why some think they don't need it:
"I feel closer to God walking in the woods
than in a building full of hypocrites."
"Sundays are the only time I can sleep in and
relax with my family."

WORSHIPING GOD IN THE WOODS is certainly a time-honored method of meditation. But it provides few evangelistic opportunities, and no fellowship (squirrels don't count).

Christians come together in worship and service to fulfill what God has called us to do. Through the power of the Holy Spirit, we are to help people learn to live their lives focused on God instead of on themselves.

"We are called to be a people to serve God, and it is tough to be a *people* by yourself," said Randall Davey, a pastor in Fairview Village, Pa. "We are who we are in a community, not in isolation."

The gathering of the church is one of the ways God shows how all-inclusive His love is, according to Davey.

"Our culture is one of selectivity, where we do things and go places with people who are like us," Davey says. "We're very choosy about who we want to be with. But the church brings about a diversity that we otherwise would not experience. We gather with people from whom we would typically withhold our grace. And when we worship as this diverse group we are struck with how profound and wide-reaching the grace of God is. These are people for whom Christ died. That is what we have in common, and that is what we celebrate together as a church."

As for the hypocrisy question, Davey has a simple answer.

"I know that there is a difference between what I *should* eat and what I eat. Everyone has those kinds of issues. But the point of being together in church is to admit our faults and collectively work toward becoming what God intended for us."

God set up the church to make His invisible, spiritual kingdom visible and physical. The church is to serve as a witness to the world that Jesus is alive. And it is to provide fellowship for believers at a deep, spiritual level—beyond the kind of fellowship available through civic groups. Christian fellowship is based on the common experience of knowing Christ personally, and on the shared desire of wanting to know Him even better.

The Wrong Reasons to Go to Church

Denver Dodrill, pastor of Kenney Memorial Wesleyan Church in Athens, Ohio, says, "There are people who attend church for the wrong reasons, such as coming only to 'get' something out of the service.

"The true disciples aren't coming to church looking for a handout. They are there to give their gifts in service to others."

Sometimes people attend church looking for a good feeling, he said.

"I can get a good feeling by watching a basketball game or hearing a great song," he said. "We should attend church to be challenged by the truth, which doesn't always feel good."

A prominent Los Angeles-area church took out a full-page advertisement in the *Los Angeles Times* that apparently tried to attract people who were looking for a bargain. In addition to a banner across the top corner of the ad that celebrated the church's free parking was this statement: "Remember, It Doesn't Cost Anything to Go to Church!"

In a culture so focused on consumerism, perhaps this advertisement fits—church is a good "value." But this doesn't fit the description of the church found in the Bible.

The early Christian church was not just a Sunday gathering, nor was it merely a support group for persecuted believers. It was a way of life.

The people lived in such a Christlike fashion that their entire lives, even their finances, were dedicated to showing that they loved others.

"They devoted themselves to the apostles' teaching and to the fellowship, to the breaking of bread and to prayer. Everyone was filled with awe, and many wonders and miraculous signs were done by the apostles. All the believers were together and had everything in common. Selling their possessions and goods, they gave to anyone as he had need. Every day they continued to meet together in the temple courts. They broke bread in their homes and ate together with glad and sincere hearts, praising God and enjoying the favor of all the people. And the Lord added to their number daily those who were being saved" (Acts 2:42-47).

Though it may not be possible to re-create this kind of arrangement in some cultures, the emphasis on eating meals together, prayer, using personal resources to meet needs, using our spiritual gifts, and praising God are all part of what the church should be today.

What Jesus Expects of the Church

Jesus described the church as His bride—the object of

His love, attention, and commitment. But He also described it as branches in a vineyard, with himself being the Vine.

He used this image to show that Christians, nourished and connected to one another by Him, depend on both Him and on one another.

The apostle Paul added another illustration to express the interdependence in the church. He called the church the Body of Christ, with Jesus as the Head and the believers as the other parts. Each part of the spiritual Body is unique, as are parts of the human body. Each part serves a function only that member could serve.

In his letter to the Ephesians, Paul gave guidelines about what the Body of Christ should do. He wrote that, although we are saved by grace through faith, we have been "created in Christ Jesus to do good works, which God prepared in advance for us to do" (2:10).

He added that the members of the Body of Christ should be patient and loving toward each other, keeping "the unity of the Spirit through the bond of peace" (Eph. 4:3). And he said if the church speaks "the truth in love, we will in all things grow up into him who is the Head, that is, Christ. From him the whole body, joined and held together by every supporting ligament, grows and builds itself up in love, as each part does its work" (vv. 15-16).

John Wesley, the father of Wesleyan theology, taught in the late 1700s that two important priorities for the church were evangelism and holy living. But leaders of the American Holiness Movement in the 1800s said the church had gotten away from holy living and that its main purpose should be the purification of the existing church through personal holiness. They continued to emphasize evangelism, though giving it a lower priority. During the early 1900s, Holiness churches shifted back to evangelism, emphasizing revivals. And today there seems to be a combined emphasis on salvation and holy living.

Local churches in Wesleyan denominations have a lot of autonomy, though, so some see their purposes more specifically toward sanctified living, some toward evangelism, some toward church growth, some toward outreach, some toward social justice, and some toward a combination of these.

A Church That Helps Their School District

At the Olive Knolls Church of the Nazarene in Bakersfield, Calif., the church sees one of its roles as influencing the city—specifically the educational system. Members of the pastoral staff travel to Holiness colleges around the country and interview potential teachers for the Bakersfield School District.

The church then helps arrange an interview with the school administration, helps pay for transportation to the interview, provides a room and meals at church members' houses, and assists in moving people to town when they are offered jobs.

This idea began in the 1960s with the pastor, Bert Rhodes, offering to help a Pasadena College quartet member find a job. Now the church does this on a regular basis and has a tremendous reputation with the school district. In one recent year, 14 of the Olive Knolls prospects were hired as teachers. In one five-year period, 40 were hired. The average is now 8 to 10 new hires a year through the Olive Knolls church.

Mel Rich, pastor of Olive Knolls, said, "I could tell you that this started because Bert saw it as a more productive way to get Christian influence in schools than by marching to protest textbooks or lobbying to get Christians on school boards.

"While that has been the result in a very low-key but powerful way, the real reason it began was that Bert had compassion on this musician who needed a job. And it blossomed from there."

Since Bert Rhodes' death, the church constructed a building named for him and offers outreach athletic leagues, counseling services, basketball camps, and weekend evening activities—all designed to minister to the needs of the city, not just to the needs of the church members.

The athletic team leaders are Christians and go through a Christian leadership development program with the pastor. "Our leagues are more than sweating and seeing who we can beat in a game," said Rich. "This is part of equipping people for service to God, which is one purpose of the church."

Though the local congregation and minister may determine the specific direction of individual congregations, their foundation is the same. They all believe that Jesus Christ is Lord of their lives and that Christians should try always to become more like Him. This means the church is growing in faith and knowledge of God through reading Scripture, prayer, praise, service, contemplation, and fellowship.

The Church Contradictory

Because there are so many dimensions to the church, descriptions of it can appear contradictory. Consider the following, for example.

Divine and Human. The church is divine because Jesus brought it into existence through His death on the Cross. Yet the church is human because it is made up of human beings with weaknesses and limitations, existing in a sinful world.

This means the church can accomplish great things, but with all these humans around, it can get caught up in great conflict. Almost everyone who has been involved in a church can remember some time when things went sour and people got hurt. Belonging to a church doesn't automatically change people into saints who know the will of God in every situation. People still are capable of sinning and making bad judgments. Yet it is the church that Jesus has chosen to carry out His message.

Visible and Invisible. Preachers, teachers, and writers have also described the church as visible and invisible. We cannot see the spiritual relationship of a person with Christ; in this sense the church is invisible. But we can see a visible church full of human beings who have that spiritual relationship.

Fighting and Victorious. The church is triumphant because the victory over sin and death has been won through Jesus. He said, "It is finished," as He died on the Cross. And our victory is assured. Yet, in the meantime, the church continues to fight sin and to lead more people to Jesus.

Universal and Local. A congregation that gathers somewhere to sing and pray is the "local" church. Everyone who belongs to Jesus Christ makes up the universal, or worldwide, church. Get these congregations together and you'd have quite a mix of people worshiping a lot of different ways.

A confused believer in China wrote to a missionary because the believer had been taught to pray with her hands stretched out, as if she were receiving a gift. She went to another church that said she was doing it all wrong, because her palms needed to be facing the ground, as if to say she was releasing everything to God.

"Which one is right?" she asked. Of course, either one would do just fine. The common factor of local churches is that Jesus is Lord and that He is moving through His creation to bring us all back to a right relationship with Him.

A Helping Hand

One of the unique insights of Holiness churches at the beginning of this century is they saw that Jesus' ministry was to the poor, as He announced to a congregation during a sermon.

"The Spirit of the Lord is on me, because he has anointed me to preach good news to the poor. He has sent me to proclaim freedom for the prisoners and recovery of sight for the blind, to release the oppressed" (Luke 4:18; see also Isa. 61:1).

Phineas Bresee, one of the leaders of the Holiness Movement in this country and a founder of the Church of the Nazarene, wrote in the first issue of his monthly paper, the *Peniel Herald*, "Our first work is to try to reach the unchurched. The people from the homes and the street where the light from the churches does not reach, or penetrates but little. Especially to gather the poor to the cross, by bringing to bear upon them Christian sympathy and helpfulness."

He added, "It is also our work to preach and teach the gospel of full salvation; to show forth the blessed privileges of believers in Jesus Christ, to be made holy and thus perfect in love."

The purpose of the church, as far as Bresee was concerned, was primarily to focus on those outside the church.

When the congregation from a Holiness church in San Jose, Calif., was looking for a pastor a few years ago, a candidate for the position was impressed with their willingness to be the kind of church Bresee would have appreciated—the kind of church God intended. During the interview with the candidate, the members repeatedly said they were concerned about friends and family members who were unsaved. They wanted their teenagers to develop sound Christian principles. They affirmed each other, laughed a lot, and were unpretentious and loving.

The candidate saw a church that believed in being an evangelistic force that would nurture believers into a holy lifestyle so that the believers would, in turn, show Christ's characteristics to the community around them. He took the position and has participated with the congregation as they led many people to Christ and started three ethnic churches.

It is possible to be a Christian and not be a part of a church. But as we become more like Christ, we grow in our awareness of our responsibility to others—both to believers and nonbelievers.

As the kingdom of God takes root in our lives, we see that, with all of its human shortcomings, the church is Christ's Body. The people who have died to self-centeredness and awakened to Christ-centeredness become aware that they are members of that Body.

Together, the members show the world what God is like. When the church focuses on living and proclaiming God's characteristics, the rest of the world is drawn to the Kingdom, fulfilling Jesus' prayer for future disciples.

"I pray also for those who will believe in me through their message, that all of them may be one, Father, just as you are in me and I am in you. May they also be in us so that the world may believe that you have sent me" (John 17:20-21).

The Short Course

Communion (Lord's Supper)

This regular part of our church schedule is far from a liturgical routine. On the contrary, this worship practice is an important way God uses to keep the conversion process alive, proclaiming His grace.

Bible Study

Wesleyan forefather John Wesley summed up how important it is to read the Bible: "Here then I am, far from the busy ways of men. I sit down alone: only God is here. In His presence I read His book; for this end, to find the way to heaven."

BACKGROUND
SCRIPTURE:
Luke 22:15-20
1 Thess. 5:16-18
2 Tim. 3:14-17
Eph. 2:1-10

Don Dunnington
and
Vicki Hesterman

Prayer

Through talking honestly with God, we come to understand His plan for our lives and are changed from the inside out.

11

How God Gives Grace

Communion, Bible study, and prayer aren't things we do to convince God we're worthy of His help. They are places we encounter God, who gives His help freely.

JULIE was an intelligent, sensitive young woman whom chapter contributor Don Dunnington met when he was chaplain at Trevecca Nazarene College. She trusted in Christ, knew her sins were forgiven, and that she belonged to the family of God. But she felt like she needed to be doing more.

She had been baptized into the body of believers, her life was committed to the Lord, and the Holy Spirit was active in her. Yet sensing there was more to being a Christian she asked her chaplain, "What do I need to do to grow in my Christian life?"

Julie's question is a common one that Christians have pondered over the centuries.

There are a lot of helpful ways we could approach these questions. But since we belong to denominations that grew out of biblical teachings rediscovered by John Wesley, let's take a look at how he might answer.

When he dealt with this issue back in the 1700s, he often used the phrase the *means of grace*. By *grace* Wesley was referring to the favor God shows to people through His love and help. We don't earn it; God freely gives it. By *means of grace* he was talking about methods God uses to deliver that life-changing grace.

The means of grace are experiences like baptism, worship, and the Lord's Supper; they were taught and modeled by Jesus. We need to learn about them and practice them because they were designed to help people live in close relationship with God. They are the spiritual disciplines Christians have used for centuries to express their faith in God and to receive God's grace for their lives.

In Wesley's sermon "The Means of Grace," he described them as outward signs, words, or actions appointed by God to serve as avenues through which He delivers grace to us.

But Wesley was quick to say we do not practice the means of grace to earn a right relationship with God. We are made right with God through faith in Jesus Christ. Only through God's grace are we saved, and not through our good works or religious practices (Eph. 2:8-9). Our participation in the means of grace is simply to place ourselves in the way of grace. It's like a thirsty Julie placing herself in front of a water fountain instead of in the middle of a desert.

We use these means designed by Christ and the church to place ourselves before Him so that He can do His transforming work in our lives.

There are a lot of spiritual disciplines, or means of grace, we could talk about. But Wesley's famous sermon on the subject highlighted the Lord's Supper, prayer, and Bible study.

The Supper That Says Grace

Wesley put special attention on the believer's participation in the Lord's Supper. He viewed holy Communion as a means of grace essential to keeping the conversion process alive.

He said, "Let every one . . . who has either any desire to please God, or any love of His own soul, obey God and consult the good of his own soul, by communicating [taking Communion] every time he can."

The Lord's Supper signified at least three things to Wesley: (1) It is a memorial meal, directing our minds back to the once-and-for-all act of redemption of Christ, who said "do this in remembrance of me" (Luke 22:19). (2) It brings us into contact with the risen Christ, truly and uniquely present through the Spirit when we participate in the sacrament. (3) It reminds us of the promise of the future glory awaiting Christians at the heavenly banquet.

Wesley declared, "Is not the eating of that bread and the drinking of that cup the outward, visible means whereby God conveys into our souls all that spiritual grace, that righteousness, and peace and joy in the Holy Ghost, which were purchased by the body of Christ once broken, and the blood of Christ once shed for us? Let all, therefore, who truly desire the grace of God, eat of that bread and drink of that cup."

Some Christians worry about the biblical warning not to take Communion "unworthily" (1 Cor. 11:27, KJV). Paul's caution was to remind the Corinthians that the Lord's Supper is to be shared by believers who have no hatred, bitterness, or improper attitudes toward others, and who come to the table with reverence and appreciation for the spiritual importance of Communion. That was apparently not happening in Corinth.

This caution does not mean sincere Christians who may feel they have failed the Lord in some way should avoid Communion.

On the contrary, repentant Christians should come to the table, recognizing forgiveness is always available. For it is during Communion that we can uniquely experience the grace of God in the presence of Christ.

When we receive the elements of Communion, it is a sign we have received the grace available through the broken body of our Lord. It is also our pledge of faithfulness to Christ, identifying us as one of His followers.

To most unbelievers, Communion means nothing. But for a Christian, it is a way into the presence of Christ.

Finding Grace in the Bible

Bible study is also a means of grace. "All who desire the grace of God," wrote Wesley, "are to wait for it in searching the Scriptures."

Searching the Scriptures means reading them, listening to others talk about them, and thinking about them. We do this to allow God to mold us more and more into the likeness of Christ.

Timothy's mentor put it well: "Continue in what you have learned and have become convinced of, because you know those from whom you learned it, and how from infancy you have known the holy Scriptures, which are able to make you wise for salvation through faith in Christ Jesus. All Scripture is God-breathed and is useful for teaching, rebuking, correcting and training in righteousness, so that the man of God may be thoroughly equipped for every good work" (2 Tim. 3:14-17).

We Christians who want to grow closer to God and become more like Christ need to allow ourselves to be shaped by God's Word. The Scripture must be worked into the whole fabric of our lives and become the basis for our thinking, feeling, and actions. For this to happen, we need to learn to read not just for information but for transformation.

Lynn was an adventurous, happy young woman who didn't think too much about the Bible when she wasn't in church. To her, an Ohio school teacher, the Bible was something preachers talked about on Sunday, not a guidance manual for the rest of the week. After college, she moved to California, far from family and friends. One Sunday, she visited a local church. Before the morning was over, she accepted an invitation to a young adult Bible study.

Lynn said those studies changed her life. She said she began to see that the Bible had practical applications to everyday life and that walking with the Lord was a personal thing. Living the Christian life wasn't something you did only on Sundays, she realized. Although she was raised by godly parents and had gone to church for years, Lynn hadn't met the Lord personally.

She finally began to understand what it meant to weave biblical wisdom into each day of her life. Lynn continued to experience God's transforming grace and to accept the deeper working of the Holy Spirit in her life. The desire to learn more about the Lord and to follow His path became a passionate part of her life. God slowly, steadily, and radically changed her.

"I grew to feel a strong desire to serve Him, to study the Bible, to become more Christlike, and to seek His will for my life," she said.

"I began to openly share relevant scripture with others who struggled or sought growth. Being a Christian was no longer a separate part of my life; it became the defining factor of who I was. Some of my friends were at first puzzled and sometimes put off. Some have since experienced similar awakenings. It is especially meaningful to pray and worship with these friends."

God's Word influenced Wesley's life in a remarkable way too. Wesley was well read on many subjects, but he continually referred to himself as a "man of one book." Even though he published about 600 works on various subjects, from medicine to politics, he wrote most about the Bible, which he considered the main source of spiritual direction. In the preface to his *Standard Sermons*, he wrote:

"O give me that book! At any price, give me the book of God . . . here is knowledge enough for me."

To allow the Bible to become the means of grace God intended it to be, there are at least three ways to read it.

1. Worshipfully. Approach it in an unhurried, reverent manner. Read to encounter God. The amount we read is not so important as the manner in which we read. Wesley wrote: "Here then I am, far from the busy ways of men. I sit down alone: only God is here. In His presence I read His book; for this end, to find the way to heaven."

2. Systematically. Follow some pattern of reading that allows you to become familiar with the grand context of Scripture, to become acquainted with the overall story line of the Old and New Testaments. By careful, planned reading you will develop knowledge of all Scripture instead of focusing just on your favorite parts.

3. As on a quest. Seek to encounter God's truth for your life and then look for ways to apply what you have discovered. Examine your life by what you are reading. For example, when you read Jesus' teaching about loving your neighbor as yourself, pause long enough to ask: How have I practiced loving my neighbor? When did I last do something in an attempt to fulfill this teaching? Do my attitudes reflect the love for others that Jesus talks about?

Prayer Takes Us to God

Wesley called prayer "the grand means of drawing near to God."

Jesus prayed and left instructions to help us learn to pray—the Lord's Prayer is a beautiful example.

We know prayer is important. Yet, it is still hard for some of us to develop a satisfactory life of prayer. The very mention of prayer often generates feelings of guilt. We feel bad either because we think we are not praying enough or are not praying in the right way.

Instead of letting guilt paralyze us, we should confess to the Lord our desire to personally know Him. We can admit our failures and misunderstandings and join the disciples in requesting, "Lord, teach us to pray" (Luke 11:1).

Learning to pray means just that—prayer is something we learn.

First, we need to learn what prayer is. Linda, a Midwestern mother of four, says she recalls learning what prayer is *not.* She made the discovery while baby-sitting neighbor children when she was a teenager.

"Every night, without fail, those kids recited six or seven prayers before they went to sleep. It took about 15 minutes, and they raced right through them. I don't think they had any idea what they were saying. I decided when I had kids that prayer would be something more meaningful, not just recitations and not just wish lists."

Linda and her children talk about who needs prayer, and they take turns praying for others. They thank God for special people and blessings. And they say a special written prayer for protection: "Jesus, tender Shepherd, hear us. Bless Thy little lambs tonight. Through the darkness be Thou near us. Keep us safe 'til morning light." This prayer, she says, gives her a chance to talk with the children about God's care.

Prayer is not just words we say to God. It is more than a mindless repetition of memorized verse, performed like a chore. It involves giving loving attention to God in every dimension of our life.

The proof of the value of prayer is not so much in documenting specific "answered prayers" as it is in how much our lives are being inwardly and outwardly transformed into the image of Christ.

Second, we need to communicate with God openly, honestly, and directly. We shouldn't worry if we can't pray as "eloquently" as a pastor. We are not supposed to pray like someone else. God wants us to come before Him in personal ways that express our deepest needs, hopes, and understandings. Our whole life should be open to Him. No secrets.

Third, we need to pray throughout the day. Call your mind to prayer as you go through your daily activities. This comes close to Paul's instructions to the early Christians to "be joyful always; pray continually; give thanks in all circumstances" (1 Thess. 5:16-18). He didn't mean we should buy knee pads so that we could spend all our time in a formal prayer posture. He meant we should learn the secret of prayerful living, of bringing everything, moment by moment, into God's presence.

Though we have talked about the three means of grace discussed by John Wesley in his famous sermon on the subject, there are many other spiritual disciplines we can practice that open our lives to the transforming work of God's grace. Worship services, fasting, solitude and reflection, small-group accountability, simplicity, and Christian service are a few other ways God can use to bring our lives into greater conformity to the image of Christ.

Simply practicing these disciplines, however, can't produce the transformation we desire. It is God who changes us. We turn to these disciplines only in obedience to God, seeking Him and knowing that He alone can make our lives all He designs them to be.

The Short Course

What It Is

Faith is basing our beliefs and actions on unseen realities. The Bible puts it this way, "Faith is being sure of what we hope for and certain of what we do not see" (Heb. 11:1). It's like not being able to swim, and jumping for the first time into the deep end of the pool, expecting Dad or Mom to catch us. They've never caught us before, but their consistent expressions of love lead us to believe and act as though they'll not let us drown.

What It Isn't

It's not just something we have, but it's also something we do—and keep doing for the rest of our life. Because faith is a journey, not a destination, Wesleyan forefather John Wesley prayed each night before retiring, "For this day, Oh Lord, do I need the merits of Thine atonement."

BACKGROUND
SCRIPTURE:
Heb. 11:1-40
James 1:2-4

Wes Harmon,
Vicki Hesterman,
and
Dean Nelson

How It Grows

Often through sufferings and failures. "Consider it pure joy, my brothers, whenever you face trials of many kinds, because you know that the testing of your faith develops perseverance" (James 1:2-3).

12

How to Have Faith

By faith, the waters of the Red Sea parted to reveal dry land. And by faith, the solid walls of Jericho came crashing down. Yet for many people today, the big question is: Can I make it through another day?

CHILDREN can be great at teaching us what faith is.

A few years ago, Dean Nelson, one of the writers of this chapter, took his four-year-old boy to the community swimming pool in Athens, Ohio. The boy, Blake, could not swim, so he played at the shallow end of the pool. But from there he watched as a steady stream of children jumped off the diving board at the other end, fell a few feet, made a big splash, remained submerged for a few seconds, emerged laughing, and swam to the side.

"I want to go off the board," Blake said.

"OK," Nelson said. "I will get in the water and catch you." Blake walked around the edge of the pool, got in line for the diving board, and Nelson swam to the deep end to tread water and wait for his son.

The boy walked tentatively out to the edge and looked over for his dad.

"Go ahead and jump," Nelson said as he prepared himself for the catch.

Blake jumped with a huge smile on his face.

Now *that's* faith. Blake had never done this before, yet he had supreme confidence that it would all work out.

The analogy breaks down a bit here, though. Nelson only thought he could catch his son. The problem was that the boy didn't jump into his dad's hands, he jumped squarely on top of his dad's head, driving the surprised father to the bottom of the 12-foot depth.

Nelson, scrambling to keep his son and himself from drowning, thrashed about, arms holding the boy aloft, legs kicking wildly to return to the surface for some life-sustaining air.

This got the attention of the pool's lifeguard who jumped in, helped the two to the side, and then banished them from the pool for breaking the rules. You're allowed to go to the deep end only if you know how to swim. It was obvious to the lifeguard that neither of the two did.

In spite of the breakdown in the analogy, there was faith in Blake's plunge into the water. The boy knew that his dad had always protected him, and, even though he had not jumped to his dad in deep water before, there was no evidence that this situation would be any different.

In the same way, we Christians base our beliefs and actions on unseen realities, taking the next steps of life without really knowing where they will lead. What we do know is that accompanying us will be the presence of God.

The Bible's Examples of Faith

The 11th chapter of Hebrews contains a dramatic account of people who lived lives of faith—people who lived in obedience to God instead of concentrating on the circumstances around them.

- By faith Abraham left his home in what is now Iraq, not knowing where he would go. After a journey of about 1,000 miles, he ended up in what is now Israel.
- By faith Sarah conceived a child, at age 90.
- By faith Abraham—at God's command—was will-

ing to offer as a sacrifice Isaac his only son, even though this seemed to doom God's promise of giving him a host of descendants.

- By faith Moses preferred to live a life of hardship with God's people rather than to live in Pharaoh's house.
- By faith God's people escaped the pursuing Egyptians by walking through the Red Sea.
- By faith the walls of Jericho collapsed.
- By faith the prostitute Rahab escaped harm because she helped God's people.

The writer of Hebrews then mentions a host of others "Who through faith conquered kingdoms, administered justice, and gained what was promised; who shut the mouths of lions, quenched the fury of the flames, and escaped the edge of the sword; whose weakness was turned to strength; and who became powerful in battle and routed foreign armies" (11:33-34). Some of these faithful did not see victory over adversity in this life, yet they persevered into the next life with the Father.

Then, as today, faith is living out the revelation and promises of God. The direction our lives seem to be going might not look clear to us. In fact, we might find ourselves confused or facing apparent contradictions, as Abraham did. But our assurance is that the presence of God surrounds us.

In his book *Faith for the Journey*, Reuben Welch points out that faith is defined by behavior, by the way choices are made and values are expressed. "Faith is how we walk, how we listen, and how we build," he says. "It is hearing when we are called, and obeying when it is time to go." Faith is not something we have, but something we do, Welch says.

Scripture as well as experience shows that the life of faith is an awakening that helps us accept God's strength to proceed despite the circumstances. And it gives us the courage even to step into the unknown.

Faith That Lives When Loved Ones Die

Joanne (Spencer) Crain knows about stepping into the unknown. In February 1981 her husband, Dean Spencer, called her from the airplane he was flying and said he would be home soon. That was their last conversation. Dean and two other businessmen died when the plane crashed into the fog-covered runway of the Pontiac, Mich., airport. Dean and Joanne had been married for 17 years, and they had three girls—Michelle, 12, and Sheri and Shannon, both 9.

"The second morning after the accident it finally settled in on me that it was all true," Joanne said. "I went into Dean's office at the house and had a fit of anger with God." Once she finished, she said an overwhelming peace came into the room, with an assurance that said, "I understand, and I will take care of you."

She said she still was frightened about the future of her family, but the assurance continued and seemed to say, "Don't look forward years or days—just five minutes at a time."

It has not been an easy life for Joanne and the girls since the tragedy. But the presence of God in their lives has been constant.

"I keep going back to that time when God assured me," Joanne said.

Just before Dean Spencer died, his book, *God Never Said We'd Be Leading at the Half,* was published, and in that book is a chapter about increasing one's faith. Rom. 10:17 says, "Faith is awakened by the message, and the message that awakens it comes through the word of Christ" (NEB). This prompted a question from Dean Spencer in his book: "Does that mean my lack of faith is caused by my lack of

reading God's Word and listening to Him? It surely does
. . . I am learning that I can increase my capacity of faith by
stepping up my input of God's Word."

When faced with difficult decisions and circumstances
after Dean's death, Joanne said she depended on her
knowledge of God's promises.

"I just believed Him," she said.

As is evident with Joanne Crain, the life of faith does
not mean all questions are answered and all doubts removed. In fact, the doubts may only be heightened. Yet,
somehow, the presence of God purifies the doubts, and actually uses them to help us in our life of faith.

Rita Roberts Waggoner, a Wheaton College student in
the 1970s, recalls an incident that showed faith amid doubt
in the life of one of her professors on the Christian campus.
Here is how she put it for *Wheaton Alumni* magazine:

> I expected college professors to stand before me as
> great intellectual generals, commanding my attention
> and inspiring me to go out into academic battle, proving
> the indisputable truths of the faith. Into this classroom of
> eagerly devout recruits came a different sort of man.
> Looking out at us with watery brown eyes, fumbling as
> he placed three frayed books on the metal desk, he began
> to speak in a low voice, hoarse from emotion.
>
> It was only this past August, he said, when his son
> —who would have been a classmate of mine—had his
> life stolen by an illness that had sapped his strength for a
> year. I waited for Dr. Erwin Rudolph to assume the pro-
> fessional role and to assure me of Divine Providence in
> Zeke's death. But instead of a preacher's voice booming
> reassurance that would echo off the walls, I heard the po-
> et's voice acknowledging the fear of nothingness.
>
> "I have a sinne* of feare," Dr. Rudolph said, quoting
> 17th-century English poet John Donne, "That when I

---

*Sin; sinne is the Old English spelling.

have spunne/My last thread, I shall perish on the shore."
Dr. Rudolph sighed, "I have a fear that there is nothing
after we die; that Zeke is gone forever."

A silence followed. We were all embarrassed by his
grief, confused by his uncertainty. Our own shadowy
fears of non-being were called forth in the poet's words.
We looked away, dropped our pencils, fidgeted with our
notebooks.

But then, Dr. Rudolph did the unexpected. He led us
in prayer. Although I no longer remember the words of
that prayer, I was embraced by this tender man's faith. I
was touched by this one who could not see his God in
the darkness, but who called out to his God nonetheless.
I heard this man who spoke of unbearable sadness and
prayed as an act of unspeakable hope.

The God I have come to know through the voices of
the Psalmist, of John Donne, of Dr. Rudolph, is a God
who embraces all of life. Our sufferings and failures are
not mere lessons to be learned, steps in some heavenly
self-improvement course. But our dark seasons of confusion are as much a part of our faith as the cross is a part
of the empty tomb.

I learned from Dr. Rudolph that our doubts do not
need to be resolved for us to act in faith; that God's presence endures even when we are isolated by our grief,
crying out that we had been forsaken. That God walks
with us in the Valley of our death and in the Shadow of
our doubt.

Faith Is a Journey, Not a Destination

Wesleyans teach that the life of faith is a journey toward
becoming like Christ. When we are saved and begin the life
of holiness, through the grace of God we are restored to
what is lacking of His image in us. Through the Holy Spirit
we can then begin to live our lives as He originally intended, a life of growing and achieving His likeness.

But when we commit to living a life of faith, we have
not arrived at the finish line. We have started. Faith is the

continuous product of God's grace and our obedience, in the midst of the circumstances of this world.

Paul's letter to the Philippians urges them to continue to "work out your salvation with fear and trembling" (2:12). The Greek term for "work out" implies continuous growth. For Paul, the life of faith is a forward look. He rejoices in what is ahead. He knows love, but he wants to know the love of Christ. He has joy, but he wants to achieve the joy of Christ. He knows *about* Christ, both by description and acquaintance, but he wants to *know* Christ intimately, to conform to His character, His relationship with the Father God, and His personhood. Paul, in his life of faith, wants to be totally identified with the likeness of Christ. And he sees this as the most worthy goal anyone could achieve.

Yet Paul never says, "I have achieved it—I have the likeness of Christ." Nor should we assume that we have "arrived." The Wesleyan tradition maintains that the fullness of the of the likeness of Christ will not appear until the journey of faith and growth has completed its course, and we have moved from an earthly to a heavenly existence. (Although at any moment we may be as "perfect" or "complete" as we can be at that moment.)

The life of faith, the journey of holiness toward becoming like Christ, will include stumbling blocks to spiritual growth. Because we are human, weaknesses, mistakes, poor judgment, and sin may occur. With this knowledge, John Wesley, our theological forefather, prayed each night before retiring, "For this day, Oh Lord, do I need the merits of Thine atonement."

The marvelous nature of the life of faith, though, is that God can use even our weaknesses to increase our faith and make us more Christlike. James tells us, "Consider it pure joy, my brothers, whenever you face trials of many kinds, because you know that the testing of your faith develops perseverance. Perseverance must finish its work so that you may be mature and complete, not lacking anything" (1:2-4).

This, then, is the life of faith: jumping off diving boards into deep water, remembering the history of God's involvement with His people, allowing God to assure us in the midst of tragedy, pressing on toward the goal of becoming like Christ, accepting failure and allowing God to use it to increase our faith, and realizing that knowledge of God and growth is increased through hearing God's Word.

Christians living this life of faith can endure pleasure and pain, victory and loss, doubt and assurance, life and death, moving and being still. For whatever happens, we can know that God is with us, loving and protecting us as only He can.

The Short Course

Rules

Growing Christians do not simply obey rules; they live out the results of being new creations in Christ.

Godly Principles

Christians emphasize the timeless principles for living found in the Ten Commandments and in the teachings of Jesus—teachings that call us to help the helpless and to treat with kindness even those who do not treat us with kindness.

Key Questions

For guidance in holy living, ask yourself these questions before making decisions: Will this compromise my faith? What would Christ do? How will this affect others? How will it affect me? Is it fair? Is it reasonable?

BACKGROUND
SCRIPTURE:
Mic. 6:8
Luke 18:18-23
John 13:34-35
Phil. 2:5-8

Dennis Bratcher
and
Dean Nelson

13

How to Live Holy Lives

Sometimes even Christians don't know how to go about deciding what's holy and what's not. They may make important decisions on the basis of what feels right or what works.

AT THE SAN DIEGO PUBLIC SCHOOL where chapter contributor Dean Nelson volunteered, the kindergarten girl's question seemed to come out of nowhere.

"Do you love Jesus?"

Nelson stopped doling out the paint to the other kindergartners for a moment, then replied, "Yes, Ashley, I do."

"Does your boy, Blake, love Jesus?"

"Yes, he does too. Do you?"

"Yes, I love Jesus."

Then she went back to painting. On the walk home, Nelson and his son talked about the school day.

"Did you know that Ashley loves Jesus?" Nelson asked.

"No, I didn't," Blake replied, as he looked for bugs to mash on the sidewalk. Then he added, "She doesn't act like it."

One of John Wesley's greatest contributions to the Christian faith was his rediscovery of "heart religion." This has helped people realize that their relationship with God made a difference in how they lived. Followers of Wesley's teaching "acted like" Christians; they were changed on the inside and as a result they lived that transformation on the outside.

During Wesley's day, in the 1700s, the dominant churches in England had produced a brand of religion that had become little more than a series of ritual acts performed during the church service. There was little recognizable commitment to God, at least not in any way that openly affected how people lived their lives.

Protestant churches of the time weren't much better. The tendency of many Protestants was to get people to believe the right thing rather than to call them to behave like disciples of Christ.

So for many people, Christianity had become irrelevant.

Wesley came to realize that a religion that does not affect how people live day in, and day out is not an effective religion. Wesley's reading of Scripture showed him that when people allow the transforming presence of God into their lives, they will be re-created from the inside out. In chapter 12 we saw that this continuous growth, or the lifelong process of being re-created, is a vital part of the Christian life. Not only is that growth personal and internal, but genuine heart religion will *always* result in a turning outward, affecting those around us.

Protestant Reformer Martin Luther defined *sin* as being turned in on oneself—in other words, selfishness. Following his lead, we could describe holiness as being turned outward to others. John Wesley wrote, "There is no holiness but social holiness." Jesus' encounter with the rich, young ruler of Luke 18 shows that helping others can be a prerequisite for eternal life. Jesus told the man who obeyed the rules of Judaism, "You still lack one thing. Sell everything you have and give to the poor, and you will have treasure in heaven. Then come, follow me" (v. 22).

The revival that swept England in the 1700s pushed

people beyond their Sunday rituals. It transformed how they lived the other six days. They not only *had* a heart "strangely warmed," as Wesley described it, but also *lived* it.

Some of the same tendencies that faced Wesley in 18th-century England face us today. Many people of our society don't claim to be Christian, so they feel no obligation to live a Christian lifestyle. Many others claim to be Christian but show no evidence of this in their lifestyles. For these people, there seems to be no external guideline on how to live. The only standard for decision making is: What's in it for me?

The self-centeredness of our day, or to use Luther's term, the "turned inward" tendency, has so influenced even the church that everyday decisions of how to behave are largely unrelated to God or morality. And these decisions certainly show no awareness of a self-emptying Christ who gave His very life for others.

Many people around us have been inoculated with just enough of the gospel to make them immune to the call for purity of life and for the heart of a servant, both of which lie at the core of the gospel. As writer William Temple said, "The Christian church is the one organization in the world that exists purely for the benefit of nonmembers."

So, as we come to the end of this series about Christian beliefs, let's ask the same question theologian Francis Schaeffer asked in the 1970s: How should you then live? Or we can ask it the way one of the Old Testament prophets did, "What does the LORD require of you?" (Mic. 6:8).

However we word it, the answer is that because of Christ living in us, we are to love one another. This love, given to us by the One who emptied himself on a cross, flows out from a transformed life. Loving others is not a *requirement* for a relationship with God. It is the *result*.

Holiness Beyond Rule-keeping

As soon as the subject of morality comes up, many people immediately think of rules and prohibitions. One young woman repeatedly refused to join a church even though she attended there for years. "If I join, I have to do what they say," she said.

Church membership and rules were inseparable. And rules to her meant prohibitions.

Countless others view Christianity as something that will inhibit them from doing things they enjoy. But to understand vital and dynamic Christian living only in terms of rules and prohibitions is to drastically misunderstand the nature of the gospel.

A Christian lifestyle is not merely conformity to rules but a living out of the transforming power of the gospel. A husband and wife who love each other deeply do not get up every morning and moan about the fact that they cannot commit adultery that day.

Their marriage vows are not merely rules. They are expressions of the love the two share.

Likewise, growing Christians do not simply obey rules; they live out the results of being new creations in Christ. One of the messages of Jesus' encounter with the rich, young ruler is that, yes, the man had followed all the rules, but no, he was still not following Christ. He had to live a transformed life, where the idols of wealth weren't as important, and where what he could do for others was the top priority.

So how do new creations make decisions differently than they used to? Let us make one distinction before we answer that.

There is a difference between *morals* and *ethics.* Morals are those abiding principles that are basic and universal. These principles do not change with circumstances and are the "baseline" from which all of life must be lived.

Ethics are the way we apply the unchanging moral principles to the changing, contradictory, and ambiguous circumstances of daily life.

For Christians and Jews, the Ten Commandments provide the moral basis for ethical decisions. The New Testament's reiteration of "love your neighbor as yourself" (Lev. 19:18) is also a governing moral principle.

For people in the Wesleyan Holiness tradition, ethics are the highest expression of a heart in tune with God, because it is in the interaction with other people that heart holiness is best expressed. For Holiness people, "ethics" is simply another way of saying "holy living."

A clear understanding of the moral principles and how we let them affect our daily lives is crucial for Christians who want to grow in their faith. It is also important to speak of them as *principles* rather than laws or rules. Life is too complex and fluid to be able to cover everything with rules, even if we wanted to. The Pharisees were notorious for trying to add law upon law to cover every circumstance in life. Their efforts were futile, even destructive.

We cannot hope to make rules fast enough to cover all aspects of being Christian in a rapidly changing world. So we must be able to apply the principles that guide our Christian walk during the changing circumstances of life. This ability is a sign of spiritual maturity in the believer.

How Not to Make Holy Decisions

The big question, then, is *how* do we make these ethical decisions as Christians?

But first, let's look as some common ways of making ethical decisions that are inadequate and incompatible with the Holiness tradition.

Emotion. For some people, emotion or feeling is a reliable gauge for dealing with others. The idea of, "If it feels good, do it," applies. But so does the concept that comedians have applied to Christians, "If it feels good, *don't* do it!"

This is a self-centered approach that invites us to use others to meet our own physical or emotional needs.

Expediency. Other people are more pragmatic. They make ethical decisions based on "what works." If it gets the job done, it is the right decision. This philosophy, however, would allow Christian bosses to bully their employees to higher performance. And though higher performance is generally considered a good thing, the idea of a Christian bully is incompatible with Christlikeness.

Consequences. Children, along with adults who are emotionally immature, often make decisions on the basis of whether or not it results in pain or pleasure. They avoid making decisions that bring discomfort. They won't confront a friend who needs to be confronted. They won't go out of their way to help someone else. And they consider it acceptable to do something "wrong" if they can do it without getting caught.

Regulations. Some Christians want the Bible or another authority, such as a church manual or a book of discipline, to spell out in black and white every rule that will apply to every specific situation before they can make ethical decisions. While the Bible and other church documents do provide ethical guidance, they do not and cannot contain a complete set of rules that cover all predicaments. Unfortunately, when there is no stated law or rule for a particular situation, decision-making for these kinds of people becomes frustrating. People who need a rule for every possible situation, and who have not learned to apply biblical principles in their lives, are immature decision-makers.

Situation. To have no guidelines beyond the immediate situation is to have no reference point at all.

This kind of relativism produces quotes like, "I know what is best for me," or "You don't understand my situation." The decision depends totally on what a person thinks is best in the immediate predicament.

How to Make Holy Decisions

So if those are the inadequate ways to make decisions, what are the adequate ones?

When faced with a difficult decision, here are some questions Christians can ask themselves.

Will this compromise my faith and commitment to God? If we are going to act like Christians, then we can allow no attitude we hold or anything we do to compromise our commitment to God.

What would Christ do? "Your attitude should be the same as that of Christ Jesus" (Phil. 2:5). A good test of any action is to allow the light of Christ's example to shine on it.

The potential problem is that we sometimes have a too narrow view of Jesus. We might see Him as a somber, monklike figure who avoids all pleasure, so we conclude that "good" ethics steer us away from any enjoyment of life. Yet, in the Gospels we see Jesus attending parties, laughing with children, and enjoying the company of others. He comments about beautiful flowers and buildings, and He enjoys music. Yet, He never shies away from making difficult or unpopular decisions.

How will this affect others? We live in a society dominated by individualists. This makes it hard for people to consider how their attitudes and actions can affect other people. Yet what is acceptable for the individual is not always good for the larger group.

This does not mean we must be driven by majority opinion. It does mean, however, that we cannot consider only ourselves when we act. We must take into account the needs of other people as well as the rest of creation. The heart of the Christian is not focused on personal rights but on the needs of others.

Is it fair? Justice is more than people getting what they deserve. More often, in the Bible, justice refers to fairness in treatment of those who are powerless to defend themselves against injustice.

A college student reported that he quit a badly needed summer job because the employer trained him to use high-pressure tactics to sell a product to people who did not need it and often could not afford it. People of God are called to accountability for how they have treated the powerless people around them.

How will it affect me? This is often hard to answer because we can't always tell how our actions will influence us. It is important, though, to remind ourselves that what we do does affect who we are.

Is it reasonable? Since God has created our minds and intellects, He expects us to use them to evaluate circumstances, situations, people, and the impact of our actions.

Sometimes, however, it can seem like God is leading us in ways that defy reason, although it probably happens less than we think. Reason alone is not the standard for behavior, but it is one of the major considerations.

Going the Second Mile

Much of what we have considered in this chapter has dealt with developing attitudes and making decisions in response to life's circumstances. But a lot of the Bible deals with more than just avoiding evil or responding to circumstances in an acceptable manner. The Bible calls God's people to work in the world as servants of God. We are called to go the second mile, to live out the implications of being redeemed and transformed people.

In the Gospel of John, one of the most important instructions Jesus gave His disciples was that they should "love one another. As I have loved you, so you must love one another. By this all men will know that you are my disciples, if you love one another" (John 13:34-35).

Jesus, having just washed their feet, showed His disciples the servant attitude they were to live out as His followers. They weren't just to talk about serving others—they were to do it.

The other Gospels also call for followers of Jesus to go the extra mile. Matthew talks of visiting people who are sick and in prison, of feeding the hungry, and of clothing the naked. He also tells of Jesus' teaching of tolerance and forgiveness, calling us to be *more* than fair with people who have been *less* than fair with us. Mark and Luke both tell us that Jesus went out of His way to help people who were not respected in normal society—people such as lepers, immoral women, members of other ethnic groups, the handicapped, and the poor.

Throughout both testaments, God's people are called to practice justice. In our culture this often means judging and condemning, making sure people pay for wrongs done, particularly those done to *us*. The biblical idea, however, is nearly the opposite, as is much of the Bible when it is compared to how society seems to work. We are called to make sure that *we*, as God's people, go out of our way to treat other people well, even if it means we may not be treated fairly.

In many cases, justice comes close to meaning the same thing as compassion. That is why, when Micah answers the question, "What does the Lord require of you?" His answer from God combines "act justly" and "love mercy" (6:8).

For the believer, justice and compassion mean being moved by the things that move God. Holy living reflects a heart warmed by the love of God and turned outward to love others.

When we have the heart of Christ, the world will recognize it. And people won't be surprised when we tell them we are Christians. They'll say that we "act like it."

Glossary/Index

AMERICAN HOLINESS MOVEMENT—The Holiness Movement is a term that refers to churches that stress entire sanctification. The Holiness Movement began after 1850 in a revival of interest in entire sanctification. This era was characterized by camp meetings with emphases on conversion of sinners and living sanctified lives. Most churches in the Holiness Movement consider themselves Wesleyan in their beliefs. Churches in the Holiness Movement include the Free Methodist Church, Church of the Nazarene, The Wesleyan Church, and others. *(See page 114.)*

JACOBUS ARMINIUS (*b.* 1560-*d.* 1609)—A Dutch theologian whose teachings greatly influenced John Wesley. As a pastor, he began to question some of the teachings of the form of Calvinism popular in Holland. Contrary to Dutch Calvinists, he taught that Christians could backslide, people could refuse to be saved, Christ died for everyone—not just those chosen for salvation, and people needed to remain faithful and obedient to God if they were to remain Christian. His teachings became more influential in England than in Holland.

ATONEMENT—A method of overcoming the problem of sin. In many religions, sacrifices are said to cover or cancel the effect of sin. Christians believe only the death of Jesus accomplishes true atonement for sin.

AUGUSTINE (*b.* A.D. 354-*d.* 430)—An influential Christian theologian and bishop from North Africa. He lived an immoral life during his young adult years, which may be why he emphasized the power of sin. He taught that original sin so corrupted human life that it was impossible to live a sinless life. He also taught that God chooses who will and will not be saved and that those chosen for salvation can never lose their salvation no matter what they do. His ideas were later developed by John Calvin. *(See page 35.)*

BODY OF CHRIST—A term used by the apostle Paul to describe the Church. This expression emphasizes both the unity and diversity of the Church, since a physical body has many parts that work together. The phrase also communicates the idea that the Church provides a continuing physical presence of Christ in the world. *(See pages 68-69, 114.)*

JOHN CALVIN (*b.* 1509-*d.* 1564)—A pastor and theologian who was one of the leaders in the Protestant Reformation. He emphasized the sovereignty of God and Augustine's teachings about predestination. Though he taught that God predestined some to be saved, it was his followers who took this to the next logical step—that God also predestined people to eternal damnation. A Calvinist is a person whose beliefs are influenced by this 16th-century theologian. The term usually indicates an emphasis on God's absolute control over the world. Often, the word is used to describe those who believe that once people are genuinely saved they can never backslide and lose their salvation. *(See page 35.)*

CHARISMATICS—A group of Christians who place special emphasis on receiving and exercising the gifts of the Holy Spirit. (The Greek word for "gift" is *charisma*.) Many charismatics teach that speaking in unknown tongues is the evidence necessary to prove that a person has been baptized with the Holy Spirit. The term is often used loosely to describe people in any church, Protestant or Catholic, who speak in tongues or who use an unknown prayer language. The largest charismatic denomination in the world is the Assemblies of God. Sometimes Charismatics are called Pentecostals. *(See page 68.)*

CHRISTIAN PERFECTION—Christian perfection is a term used in the Holiness Movement for entire sanctification. It means to be made perfect in love toward God and humanity. Christian perfection is the work of God's grace in the believer. Christian perfection is not total perfection. Only God is perfect in this way. It is not the perfection of angels. It is not the perfection humanity had before the Fall, nor human perfection. Christians can still make mistakes. Christian perfection allows for growth in grace. *(See pages 89-91.)*

COMMUNION—An intimate or spiritual sharing. It can be used to describe a close personal communication between God and a believer. It can also be a synonym for the Lord's Supper, since partaking of the Lord's Supper is an act of sharing a special and close communication with Christ. For John Wesley, the Lord's Supper directs our minds back to the once-and-for-all act of redemption, brings us into contact with the risen Christ, and reminds us of the promise of the glory awaiting Christians at the heavenly banquet. *(See pages 122-124.)*

DOCTRINE—The teaching of a church on theological subjects such as God, the authority of Scripture, and the Second Coming. Sometimes the word is used to describe the official teachings required for membership, such as those found in creeds and articles of faith. But doctrine is also used in an informal way to refer to the general religious opinions of a group of people. *(See page 33.)*

ENTIRE SANCTIFICATION—An expression used in Wesleyan theology to describe the act of God that makes a Christian holy in motives and actions. Entire sanctification is a crisis experience that happens after a person completely consecrates his heart to God subsequent to becoming a Christian through conversion. This experience provides cleansing from the tendency to sin. *(See pages 88, 90, 92-93, 95-98.)*

FAITH—A response of trust or confidence in our relationship to God. This is more than just belief that God is real. It speaks of acting on that belief, through a life of trust and obedience to God. *(See pages 78, 101, 130-138, 140-141, 145, 147.)*

GRACE—The undeserved mercy of God. All good things that come from God are expressions of His grace. However, the word is most often used to describe the actions of God that lead a person toward salvation or heaven. *(See pages 22-24, 27-29, 37-41, 76, 108, 120-126, 136-137.)*

HOLY—Holy describes the perfection and unity of God that are His alone. Holy also describes that which is set apart for God's use. People, days, places, and things become holy when they are set apart for God's service. These are called holy because the presence of God sanctifies them. *(See pages 47-48, 55-57, 81-82, 88-90, 97-98, 145, 147, 149.)*

HOLINESS—Complete commitment to God. In Wesleyan theology, the word also refers to a condition of victory over sin. No longer does the power of sin control our lives. *(See pages 24, 48, 87-90, 92, 136-137, 142, 144-145.)*

HUMAN NATURE—This refers to characteristics common to all human beings. The phrase may be used in two ways. It is often used to describe what human beings are by creation. They are created in the image of God and thus are free, creative, and responsible. The term is also used by some theological traditions as a synonym for sinful nature. Wesleyans understand human nature as separate from sinful nature. We are born into the world as sinful humans. In sanctification, human nature is separated from sinful nature. Although sin no longer rules the life of the believer, believers are still fully human—free, creative, responsible, as well as capable of making mistakes. *(See page 56.)*

INCARNATION—A term used to describe the event of God becoming human in the form of Jesus by taking upon himself a human body. *(See page 55.)*

INERRANCY—The teaching that the writing of the Bible was so completely controlled by God that no errors of any kind appeared in the original manuscripts. Some evangelicals say that believing this is the only way to preserve the authority of the Bible. Other evangelicals, such as many Wesleyans, believe that God did not dictate the Bible. Instead, God directed the writing of Scripture to the point that it is totally reliable in all matters of faith and salvation. *(See page 35.)*

INITIAL SANCTIFICATION—A term in Wesleyan theology used to show that a person begins enjoying a holy relationship with God at conversion. Further growth in holiness follows as a person lives the Christian life. *(See pages 81-82.)*

INSPIRATION—A word to describe the belief that God was involved in the writing of the Bible to such an extent that it can be truly called the Word of God. There are many different ideas about how this inspiration actually took place. Some say God allowed the writers freedom to express the truths in their own words and writing style. Others say God carefully selected each word. However the inspiration took place, 2 Tim. 3:16 affirms that all scriptures are inspired by God. *(See pages 34, 36-37.)*

JUSTIFICATION—Another way of talking about forgiveness. Justification is the process by which God puts people into a right relationship with himself. At the moment of conversion, God removes a person's guilt and sin, which had been obstacles that kept the individual from having a relationship with God. *(See pages 79-80, 95.)*

KINGDOM OF GOD—A phrase used by Jesus to summarize His teaching about the need for total obedience to God. It is sometimes translated "the reign of God" or "the rule of God" to show that the kingdom of God does not mean a geographical location but a relationship of obedience. *(See pages 106, 119.)*

PLENARY INSPIRATION—The word *plenary* describes something that is full or complete. So, plenary inspiration means that the whole Bible was inspired by God. The 66 books contain all that people need to know for their salvation. The Bible is complete in what it says about God, humanity, and salvation. *(See page 36.)*

MEANS OF GRACE—Avenues through which God conveys to us spiritual life and strength for daily living. These include Bible reading, prayer, fasting, worship with others, compassionate ministry, and especially the Lord's Supper. *(See page 122.)*

ORIGINAL SIN—A phrase with a twofold meaning. It refers to the first sin—committed by Adam and Eve in the Garden of Eden. It also refers to the tendency of human beings to sinfully rebel against God. *(See page 19.)*

PENTECOST—A Jewish religious festival in late May or early June, seven weeks after Passover. It was a celebration of the firstfruits of harvest. On the Pentecost after Jesus' ascension, God poured out the Holy Spirit on the disciples as they were praying in Jerusalem. Some Christians use the word to describe the coming of the Holy Spirit into people's lives.

PERFECT LOVE—Wholehearted love for God and for others. This term from 1 John 4:12-18 is used to describe how completely the love of God can permeate our lives. John Wesley described perfect love as love that expels fear. *(See pages 88-91.)*

PREVENIENT GRACE—The love of God reaching out to all people before conversion, enabling them to accept Christ as Master of their lives. The Bible teaches that salvation is not a human achievement, so it cannot begin simply as a human choice. Wesleyans teach that God gives prevenient grace to all people to allow them to respond to the gospel if they so desire. *(See pages 23, 27.)*

PROTESTANT—A Protestant was one who protested against errors in the Roman Catholic Church in the 1500s. Martin Luther and John Calvin were two leaders of this movement called the Reformation. They said that any beliefs not taught in Scripture should be rejected. Thus they rejected certain Roman Catholic doctrines such as purgatory and salvation through good works. Present-day Protestants stress the priesthood of all believers and the importance of Scripture over tradition. Holiness churches are included among Protestants today. *(See pages 81, 142.)*

REDEMPTION—Paying the price required to set a person free from captivity or slavery. The New Testament teaches that Jesus' death paid the required price to set believers free from slavery to sin. Though the price was paid by Jesus on the Cross, the freedom is available only when an individual believer accepts it at conversion.

REGENERATION—Another term to describe what happens when a person is saved. The word means "new birth" or being born again. *(See page 81.)*

REVELATION—The understanding that God makes himself known to human beings. This implies that we would know nothing about God had He not chosen to reveal himself to us. Some theologians speak of two kinds of revelation: general revelation refers to what we can know about God from nature, and specific revelation refers to what we can know about God from the Bible. *(See pages 30, 36-38, 47, 133.)*

SANCTIFICATION—The process by which someone or something is made holy. Becoming a holy person is not a human achievement, though it requires an attitude of trust and obedience toward God. Since sanctification is the work of God, it is an act of His divine grace. *(See pages 68, 88, 90, 96-97.)*

TRINITY—A theological term to express the biblical teaching that God is one and yet three persons: Father, Son, and Holy Spirit. Christians are left with the mystery of this oneness and threeness, for though the New Testament clearly teaches both, it doesn't explain how this could be. *(See pages 49-50.)*

CHARLES WESLEY *(b. 1707-d. 1788)*—A powerful preacher, but most famous for the more than 7,000 hymns he wrote during his lifetime. A younger brother of John Wesley, Charles shared in the Wesleyan revival of the 1700s in England. Most of his hymns were written for worship, and more than 100 of them are still used in churches today. *(See page 24.)*

JOHN WESLEY (*b.* 1703-*d.* 1791)—A British evangelist and practical theologian. Wesley emphasized that Christians should completely love God and neighbor, and should live a life of holiness. Though he remained in the Church of England all his life, he founded Methodist societies that became the Methodist Church after his death. Wesley's emphasis on holiness makes him the theological mentor for the Holiness Movement and for denominations such as the Church of the Nazarene, Free Methodist Church, and The Wesleyan Church. *(See pages 25-27, 39-40, 95, 141-142.)*

WESLEYAN—A person or idea influenced by the teaching of John Wesley. Wesleyans emphasize the importance of holiness in both motives and actions and reject the idea that Christians can't help but sin every day. They also emphasize that people are not chosen by God ahead of time for either heaven or hell but that God's gift of salvation is available to everyone who chooses to accept it. *(See pages 37-41, 79, 81-82, 88, 90, 92, 97, 105, 108, 114-115, 136-137, 145.)*

WESLEYAN-ARMINIAN—A term used to describe theology that has developed from teachings of both Jacobus Arminius (1560-1609) and John Wesley (1703-91). *(See pages 37-38.)*

WESLEYAN QUADRILATERAL—A description of the four main resources Wesleyan theologians use to develop theological understandings. These resources are Scripture, the traditional teachings of the church, reason, and human experience. Scripture is the foundational and most important basis for Wesleyan theology, but Wesleyan theologians give more weight to human experience than do theologians in some other theological groups. *(See pages 33-34.)*

WORD—A term used in John 1 as a title for Christ. It is the English translation of a Greek word, *logos,* which was used in Greek philosophy to identify the rational principle or being that controlled the world. John draws on both Greek philosophy and Old Testament understandings of the Word of God to describe Christ as the preexistent, creating Word. *(See pages 34, 54-55.)*

These definitions have been compiled from the following sources:

Hahn, Roger, Ph.D., chair of the Department of Religion and Philosophy, Southern Nazarene University, Bethany, Okla.

Truesdale, Albert, et al. *A Dictionary of the Bible and Christian Doctrine in Everyday English*. Kansas City: Beacon Hill Press of Kansas City, 1986.